ARAB NEW YORK

Arab New York

*Politics and Community in the
Everyday Lives of Arab Americans*

Emily Regan Wills

NEW YORK UNIVERSITY PRESS
New York

NEW YORK UNIVERSITY PRESS
New York
www.nyupress.org

References to Internet websites (URLs) were accurate at the time of writing. Neither the author nor New York University Press is responsible for URLs that may have expired or changed since the manuscript was prepared.

Library of Congress Cataloging-in-Publication Data
Names: Wills, Emily Regan, author.
Title: Arab New York : politics and community in the everyday
lives of Arab Americans / Emily Regan Wills.
Other titles: Politics and community in the everyday lives of Arab Americans
Description: New York : New York University Press, [2019] |
Includes bibliographical references and index.
Identifiers: LCCN 2018020901| ISBN 9781479897650 (hbk. : alk. paper) |
ISBN 9781479854875 (pbk. : alk. paper)
Subjects: LCSH: Arab Americans—New York (State)—New York—Ethnic identity. |
Arab Americans—New York (State)—New York—Political activity. | Arab Americans—
New York (State)—New York—Social conditions. | New York (N.Y.)—Ethnic relations.
Classification: LCC F128.9.A65 W55 2019 | DDC 305.892/70730747—dc23
LC record available at https://lccn.loc.gov/2018020901

New York University Press books are printed on acid-free paper, and their binding materials are chosen for strength and durability. We strive to use environmentally responsible suppliers and materials to the greatest extent possible in publishing our books.

Manufactured in the United States of America

10 9 8 7 6 5 4 3 2 1

Also available as an ebook

CONTENTS

NOTE ON ARABIC TRANSLITERATION

All Arabic words have been transliterated with an eye toward ease of reading for the non–Arabic speaker. The ع has usually been transliterated as an apostrophe, no distinction has been made between ه and ح, خ has been transliterated as *kh*, غ has been transliterated as *gh*, initial hamza has been elided, and vowels have been written with an ear toward the ability of a non–Arabic speaker to reproduce the word in a way that would be recognizable to a speaker of Levantine Arabic.

PART I

Everyday Lives

1

Everyday Politics in Arab New York

What Does It Mean to Be Arab American?

Brooklyn on a warm, early-summer morning. I was at Shore Road Park, on the waterfront in the neighborhood of Bay Ridge to help set up the annual Arab American Bazaar, alongside other volunteers and staff from the Arab American Association of New York (AAA). I worked alongside my friend Suleikha, who ran the children's activities at the AAA, setting up the craft tent; she kept a wary eye on the large stage as the twenty-two Arab flags were hung across the top, making sure that the Egyptian flag was hung properly alongside the others. Many of the volunteers around us were high school students, earning community service credit for their time; they hung out and chatted as much as they did anything useful. Slowly, a ring of booths formed around the stage: vendors selling buttons reading "Falafel Addict" or "I didn't choose to be Arab, I just got lucky"; the mom of a teenaged volunteer selling homemade Sudanese food; the ubiquitous corn-grilling and lemonade-pressing stands of every NYC summer street fair. Balady Foods, a major grocery store on Bay Ridge's Fifth Avenue (located across from the AAA's offices), set out backgammon boards, hijabs, and packaged snack foods in their booth; next to it, a mobile *argilah* (hookah) café was set up. The US Census Bureau organized a table to talk about the upcoming 2010 census, and the Brooklyn District Attorney's office was represented by an employee who was also a frequent AAA volunteer.

The Arab American Bazaar began, and people strolled in to enjoy the day. I recognized many of the women from the AAA English classes I volunteered in and others who dropped their children at the association's programs. Others were unknown to me, some of the over ten thousand Arab American residents of Bay Ridge and Sunset Park, or the over ninety-seven thousand Arab Americans who live in the five boroughs of New York City. Suleikha and I settled in to the children's tent with some of the young volunteers; we painted kids' faces and helped them color pictures of Arab flags, which they could then put on pipe cleaners to wave. On the main stage, performers sang pop hits and standards; Suleikha muttered to me after one performance, "Who knew the Yemeni falafel guy was a wedding singer?" The AAA's dance troupe of young women performed *dabke*, a Levantine folk dance performed at weddings and celebrations; another group of Egyptian dancers performed a folk dance with sticks, wearing shiny *galabiyyas* (long robes) and heavy eye makeup. In between acts, Linda Sarsour, then director of the AAA and the event's MC, encouraged people to care about the Arab community scene and introduced politicians: Bay Ridge's city councilman, state senator, and state assemblywoman, who all gave awkward but polite speeches celebrating the day. Linda was not subtle about the electoral power she saw in the crowd: "Voting is the duty of all of us who have gotten our citizenship," she said in Arabic and then repeated in English.

Among the crush of children getting their faces painted (Spider-Man was a popular choice, as were the Palestinian and Egyptian flags), their mothers trying to keep them under control, and the volunteering teenagers, I saw a young white woman holding a clipboard clasping green paper. She was one of the fleet of young people you see in the summer before an election in New York City working for candidates for city offices; each candidate must get a certain number of signatures to earn a spot on the Democratic ballot, so these young people canvass for signatures, both door-to-door and at public events. I've signed forms brought to my door in Kensington, the multiethnic transitional neighborhood where I lived, as well as at Brooklyn LGBT Pride and the Park Slope Family Street Fair. The girl with the clipboard surveyed the people standing under the tent and approached me. Very politely, she asked first if I was a registered Democrat and then whether I would sign her petition. I had already signed for this candidate, which I told her. She thanked me, handed me a brochure about him, and wandered away from the tent without asking any of the adults around me to sign. Briefly, she paused in the middle of the path among the families and groups of friends milling around on their way from the performance stage to shaded corners of the park, where they could sit and chat. After standing in the path for a minute, watching people go by, she went to the playground on the other side of the park, without asking any of the hundreds of Arab Americans around her for their signatures.

That young woman was looking for political interlocutors. She was seeking someone who could join her in her goal of getting her candidate on the ballot and eventually into office. She wanted to be able to tell people about his accomplishments and encourage them to vote for him in the September primary. Standing on that crowded park path, the only person she could recognize as someone to talk with about politics was me, easily the whitest, least Arab-looking person at the entire festival.

I don't know the motives of that young volunteer. She might have been nervous about language barriers; she might have been concerned that noncitizens might sign the petition by mistake, which could invalidate it. But this book is motivated by the general question posed by her actions: Why do so few non–Arab Americans consider Arab Americans as people they can speak with about US politics? Why can they be the targets of formal political discourses but never partners in the exchange?

One consistent finding of research on Arab American communities and an observation among many who know the community well is that most people of Arab descent in the United States are not politically mobilized as individuals or as members of groups. The Detroit Arab American Survey (DAAS) data show that Arab Americans fall lower than other Detroiters, and other Americans, in almost all categories of political participation.[1] The history of get-out-the-vote campaigns and political mobilization efforts run by national Arab American associations is one of marginal success. Few of those who might be identified as Arab American by ancestry or country of origin actively support ethnic lobbying organizations like the American-Arab Anti-Discrimination Committee. Very few people of Arab descent have ever held national-level elected office; all of those in Congress have been Christian descendants of early twentieth-century Syrian-Lebanese immigrants, none of whom have ties to current Arab immigrant communities.[2] From electoral politics to organized lobbying to civic participation, Arab Americans are not as engaged in the formal sphere of politics as their neighbors.

Yet politics is everywhere for Arab Americans: in the evaluation of when and where to trust government actors such as Homeland Security or local police forces, in feelings about the political conditions in countries and communities of origin, in high-definition televisions turned to Al Jazeera in coffee shops and restaurants, in the Palestinian flags teenagers wear on their backpacks and the demonstrations where families turn out to chant in Arabic. (The only area where the DAAS shows that Arabs participate more than non-Arabs is in attending demonstrations.) Even as the literature on formal political participation argues that Arab Americans don't participate in American politics, the literature on the Arab American experience argues that politics is omnipresent and unavoidable in Arab Americans' experiences of their social world, particularly in interactions with non–Arab Americans. While all of us are necessarily engaged with or affected by political issues merely by existing in community with others, many Arab Americans experience that politicization as compulsory, as a form of what Evelyn Shakir names as "political racism."[3]

I believe these two facts—that Arab Americans don't participate in formal politics and that politics is ever present in the Arab American lived experience—are causally linked. Because of the ways that stereotypes, prejudices, and biases constrain Arab Americans' ability to participate in American political life, coupled with the intense relevance of politics to their experiences as Americans and as Arabs, a significant portion of Arab American political practices take place outside the sphere of formal politics and remain firmly ensconced in everyday life. Therefore, if we want to understand how Arab Americans engage in politics, we have to turn to their daily practices and look there for politics, in the particular forms and shapes it takes on under those conditions.

What Does It Mean to Be Arab American?

The category "Arab American" assigns a common identity to a tremendously diverse group of people. People of Arab descent in the United States can be the descendants of the wave of Syrian-Lebanese immigrants in the late nineteenth century and early twentieth century who immigrated alongside Southern and Eastern Europeans to work as peddlers or industrial laborers, or they or their families could have immigrated after the liberalization of immigration laws in the 1960s. (Of the 1.8 million persons of Arab descent in the United States according to the American Community Survey, about a million were born in the country and 750,000 were born abroad; nearly 48 percent of those born abroad immigrated after 2000.) People who identify or are identified as Arab Americans can be Maronite, Orthodox, Coptic, or Protestant Christians; Sunni or Shi'a Muslims; Druze, Jewish, or practitioners of no religion at all. They or their families can have come from any of the Arabic-speaking countries of West Asia and North Africa and may have intermediate roots in Europe, elsewhere in Asia or Africa, or in Latin America. Arab-identified individuals can speak Arabic as a first language, through study, as a colloquial to talk with family, or a formal liturgical language; they also might not speak Arabic at all. (Of Arab-identified families in the American Community Survey, 41 percent speak English at home; of those who speak another language at home, fewer than 22 percent speak English less than "very well.") Legally, they are identified by the US government as "white," the result of advocacy by early Syrian and Lebanese immigrants seeking naturalization under anti-Asian citizenship laws. Some are read by those who see them as white; some are read as black or may identify as black; others are read as Arab or as ambiguously "nonwhite." Many but not all Arabs identify as people of color, and others dislike being subjected to racial categories altogether.

There is also the additional complication that "Arab," as a term of identity, functions as both an ethnic and a panethnic identifier. Both researchers and others usually think of ethnicities as internally coherent entities, even though they are obviously internally divided by intersecting identities and the inevitable fact of human diversity. Ethnic groups are supposed to share a common identity that cannot be subdivided. But panethnicities are "uniquely defined by an inherent tension derived from maintaining subgroup distinctions while developing a sense of metagroup unity."[4] Like "Latina/o" or "Asian," "Arab" refers to people with a wide variety of national origins, religions, races, and other identities. They share a broad region of origin and a language (though the Arabics spoken by Arabs are as diverse as the Spanishes spoken by Latina/os), but their shared identity has subcategories that remain relevant even as people belong to the panethnic category.

While understanding "Arab" as a panethnicity makes sense for diaspora communities, it is complicated by the concepts of Arab nationalism or pan-Arabism, a long-standing political discourse in Arab countries. Pan-Arabism argues that Arabic speakers form a coherent national unit distinct from other nations and that the borders between Arab states are colonial impositions that should be obliterated. While political manifestations of pan-Arabism have waned in the late twentieth and early twenty-first centuries, the general idea remains relevant. This discourse suggests that "Arab" is a coherent ethnic identity category that just happens to have members divided by geography. For most individuals who have lived in the region, it makes sense to think of all people of non-minority ethnicity from Arabic-speaking countries as a single group ("Arabs"). That means that when those individuals arrive in diaspora, they may think of Arab as an ethnicity, a single group sharing an identity, instead of as a panethnicity, a coalition of subgroups that nevertheless have an overarching shared community.

The combination of the tremendous diversity of people of Arab descent and the competing possibilities for ethnic or panethnic identification means that identifying that individuals have Arab ancestry does not, necessarily, tell us how they understand themselves. They may identify as Arab, as Muslim or Christian, as a specific nationality, as another part of their ancestry (Irish, Italian, African), as American, or as any combination of these. They may or may not consider themselves a part of an Arab community, and that affiliation may change as their experiences, broader social conditions, and personal thoughts on the matter change. They may or may not choose to participate in cultural, social, or other institutions that are identifiably Arab, regardless of how they identify.

In this book, I focus on what we might call an "Arab community in practice," meaning people who both identify themselves as Arab (which does not include every person who might have ancestry in Arab countries) and participate in community activities and institutions with other people who so identify.[5] In particular, I study clients and staff at Arab community organizations and participants in Arab-identified social movements, examining their collective work, thought, and perspectives. These are people who consider their Arab identity important, for either practical reasons (language accessibility, connections to important services) or ethical ones (feeling fulfilled in their identity, reaffirming their commitment to a meaningful narrative of self), and join together with others who share that perspective to achieve important personal or collective goals.

My research is focused in New York City, the largest and densest city in the United States. The New York City Metropolitan Statistical Area contains the third largest concentration of people of Arab descent in the United States, after Los Angeles and Detroit, including both descendants of the first immigrants to arrive in the Middle East from Arab countries in the late nineteenth century (as well as the institutions they built) and constant streams of current arrivals. New York's Arab community has not been studied as closely as the Arab community of Detroit has, despite being equally historically embedded and of fairly similar size. This book aims to both document and provide some preliminary analysis of Arab New York as a particular Arab community (or set of them) as well as to use this landscape to dig deeply into the relationships between everyday politics and Arab American community life, as seen in the particular context of a massive, multicultural, influential city's culture and practices.

Why the Everyday?

"Everyday politics" is an amorphous way of talking about political action and activity that takes place at some remove from formal political systems.[6] I use the framework of "everyday politics" as a lens to look at how interactions and activities we might not consider as "political" demonstrate how politics and contestation structure the lived experiences of Arab Americans. I look at civil society and social movement activities, not to consider the explicitly political actions they undertake but instead to consider the "nonpolitical" practices that people who come together through these activities engage in. This lens does not require that I make any judgment about whether the spaces I am observing are "inherently" political or not. For instance, social movements in general have a clear claim on being political organizations, regardless of their position outside institutionalized politics, and civil society activity and organizations have important connections and links with the state and organized political action. But this book focuses instead on the ways that people interact while engaging in activities in these spaces, how their experiences and self-articulations shape their outlook and perspectives on politics, and how their practices go on to matter to the actions and behaviors they engage in that are intended to have political meaning.

Politics is not walled off from all other aspects of people's daily existence, but is bound and intertwined with it in a variety of ways. We experience governmentality and politics in our everyday lives, and we process our experiences about them with others; we also situate our political actions within our everyday contexts, such as our interpersonal relationships, our interpretations of our own experiences and those of others like us (which first requires determining who is like us), and our social practices that reinforce particular forms of political and social action. I use an everyday politics lens because I am interested in understanding the political in ways that expand beyond merely focusing on questions of state and government. Politics is about *contestation*, the forms of struggle, disagreement, and argument that make up our social lives, and about *power*, the ability of groups or individuals to constrain the actions or contestation of others. Wherever people feel the constraint of powerful discourses or laws, and particularly wherever they struggle, argue, or resist the workings of power, I believe we have found politics. Some of these moments happen in the intersection between the state and those it governs; others happen within the state, where competing forces contest to try to control a question or issue or policy; and others happen outside of this framework altogether, where the power hierarchy between actors in a social setting becomes a limit to contestation or structures how that contestation can take place.

An emphasis on everyday politics can be used to approach many different domains of political life. (One could, for instance, do an everyday-politics analysis of a legislator's office or a site where the public encounters the government, such as a welfare office or the Department of Motor Vehicles.) However, an everyday politics lens is particularly well suited to the study of Arab American communities for a number of reasons. First, the sphere of the everyday is crucial for immigrant communities and their process of acculturation and integration into their new countries. The effects of state policies on immigrant integration, for instance, are dependent on "the social, localized nature of acquiring and practicing political citizenship."[7] In civic organizations, shared assumptions about social and political life are communicated and produced through participation, shaping immigrants into members of their broader communities.[8] And immigrant engagement in voluntary and civic organizations is most linked to formal political participation when there is a substantial amount of "political interaction and activity that transpires within the organizations with which respondents affiliate," such as discussion of political issues or taking stances on political issues.[9] The through line here is that political engagement, particularly for immigrants, is built, structured, and influenced through the sphere of the everyday. Therefore, these spaces are a key zone for studying politics at its most basic level, particularly for communities who seem politically disengaged.

Everyday politics is also an important element of social movement activity, one of the conventionally political spheres in which Arab Americans are most organized. For instance, the literature on prefiguration demonstrates how movements engage in practices both large and small, many of which are embedded in everyday life, which embody the future world, and that these prefigurative spaces are where much of the political and politicizing work of social movements takes place.[10] Social movement frameworks also emphasize how claiming space is a political process: "The point is not to create a context in which the 'real' work of a social movement can be done; the creation (and/or defense) of places is political work."[11]

In addition, analysis of identity in social movements has emphasized the centrality of the everyday. For instance, everyday practices of dress, behavior, and interaction constitute the ideological performances that render people legible and legitimate actors in social movements,[12] and daily identity performances and activities are central to participation in many social movements, particularly those that focus on identity.[13] Studying social movements only through the ways they interact with states, make formal claims, or engage in spectacular mass mobilization makes it impossible to document and trace features that have crucial impacts on how those movements are actually conducted and what results they might be able to have.

Most importantly, I believe that the sphere of the everyday is able to offer a useful lens on a matter that is crucially important to the political experiences of Arab Americans: the problems of political discourse. "Discourse" is a conceptually vexing term in political theory and in the study of politics in general. From Habermas, we get the notion of a practical discourse, an actual conversation that people have with each other where they test the validity of proposed norms.[14] Discourse is fundamentally about reason giving and argumentation in these spaces, whether they be face-to-face, in the media, or ongoing cultural contestations, and what matters is that discourse within them is carried out ethically. But from Foucault, we get the notion that discourses define relations between objects and their names and, among objects themselves, making up the structure of conceptual relations that pattern social life.[15] These discourses are always constructed by power, and the workings of power can be seen in how they assign names and relations between objects subject to them.

I envision the relationship between these two notions of discourse as an interlocking framework, creating nested sets of discourses that are a primary space for political contestation and yet are constrained and limited by the workings of power in social and political life. Participants in a practical discourse are constrained by a structuring discourse, meaning a discourse in the Foucauldian mode. Those structuring discourses limit and shape the utterances that people are able to use within practical discourses and in fact help define who is able to be a participant in those discourses and which conditions they can take within them.

Axel Honneth theorized that our sense of social injustice is driven by misrecognition: that the less we believe ourselves to be understood and recognized in the ways that are important to us, the less we feel we are being treated fairly in the world. He identifies three key spheres of recognition: the sphere of love, meaning our personal being and uniqueness as individuals; the sphere of equality, meaning our existence as deserving equal consideration and respect as members of a community; and a third sphere that he gives various names at various times, but which I would call ethical recognition, our need to be recognized as having the particular values and qualities that make us who we are and affirm our membership in ethical communities.[16] But I believe that these categories are insufficient to capture the injustice that occurs when structuring discourses limit and prevent people from being able to take part in practical discourse in key ways. This form of injustice cannot neatly fit into the categories of the spheres of love, equality, and ethical existence; it belongs elsewhere.

The term I have developed to talk about these issues is "discursive misrecognition." Discursive misrecognition is the uniting of the identity of speakers (in this case, Arab Americans) to the content of their speech (politically contentious or about issues such as terrorism, religion, or US/Middle East policy), such that certain actors are not free to take part in a practical discourse without excessive restriction. Their ability to be a part of public-sphere discussions about matters of importance to them is constrained, in part because of the content of what they might say, and in part because of who they are while saying it. This experience is not limited to Arab Americans, but it is a continual factor in the political life and speech of people who prioritize an Arab identity when engaging in public: that their attempts to talk about political issues they care about will likely fail because their speech will be met with misrecognition rather than taken as a legitimate form of participating in practical discourse.

People who are discursively misrecognized may be discouraged from speaking or told to be silent when they do speak. Alternately, they may be subject to demands for forced speech. A common example of forced speech is when Arabs or Muslims are called upon to make explicit statements that they support democracy, denounce terrorism, and pledge allegiance to the United States as a precondition for any public speech. Interlocutors may also refuse to hear or engage with a speaker's statement. (These two combine, in a particularly poisonous form, in the continued calls for Muslims to denounce Islamist terrorism that seem to assume that no Muslim leader has ever done so—when Muslims of many ideological stripes have been doing so as long as there has been Islamist violence.) Misinterpretation, or the linking of a statement made in one context to another that renders it politically poisonous, is also common. Louise Cainkar's work on Arab American experiences after the September 11 attacks details two practices that she calls "consulting the Arab mind" and "knowledge games," where Arab Americans are asked to explain why "Arabs" or "Muslims" are the way they are, or challenged repeatedly about whether their lived experience is real.[17] Each of these actions ends up misrecognizing speakers and their speech distinctly, ruling them out of the realm of persons who can take part in a practical discourse in a full and meaningful way.

What this means is that Arab Americans who openly claim such an identity are denied the ability to be full participants in practical discourses.[18] For instance, take a controversial example from the era just before I began the fieldwork for this book. Debbie Almontaser was a

New York City public school teacher and administrator who had been selected to be the principal of the newly formed Khalil Gibran International Academy, a charter middle school and the first school in the city to teach Arabic as a second language. She was asked in an interview about a T-shirt that said "NYC Intifada," produced by a group that shared office space with a Yemeni community group she was involved with. Her response was to define the word *intifada*, which means a "shaking off" of injustice and oppression, usually in the context of a political uprising or movement.

However, she was not treated as if she had explained a foreign word to those unfamiliar with it or had given context that she, as a native Arabic speaker, would be uniquely placed to share. Instead, she was interpreted as having supported violence against civilians in New York and Israel and was harassed so severely by the right-leaning press and internet communities that the Department of Education terminated her as principal of the Khalil Gibran International Academy and appointed a non-Arabic-speaking, white, Jewish principal instead. Almontaser continues to be harassed by actors on the Islamophobic right to this day. The KGIA collapsed after only a few years, owing to the structural problems of the small, themed schools run within the public school system, a loss of credibility in the eyes of many in the Arab community, and the negative publicity (the right-leaning press repeatedly called the school a *madrassa*, which is the Arabic word for school, but was intended to indicate an Islamist indoctrination program). Almontaser's treatment fundamentally violates principles of discourse ethics: she could not express herself fully, and her statement was challenged and constrained in ways that invalidated her ability to communicate, interrogate the statements of others, and defend her own positions. She was discursively misrecognized in that moment, and it undermined her ability to be a full and complete political actor.

Using an everyday politics lens, we can identify that this is not only a problem that people have when they become prominent public officials or make statements in the media or other public forums. As Habermas says, an individual "cannot extricate himself from the communicative practice of everyday life in which he is continually forced to take a position by responding yes or no."[19] We exist in the practical discourses we have with others, in the ways we negotiate social life, evaluate norms and principles, and make decisions through the process of contestation and conversation. Meanwhile, the practical discourses we engage with are constantly being shaped by the existing sets of assumptions, object relations, and limitations of thought that are common to our period in history and our positions in society. Arab Americans who attempt to participate in these discourses find themselves shut out, constrained, or limited by the structuring discourses at work in American society.

What, then, can Arab Americans who care about politics do? One strategy is to push back against discursive misrecognition directly by participating in ways that assume, demonstrate, or openly claim that Arab Americans *are* equal participants in US political discourses and to make claims on the basis of norms around equality when discursive misrecognition inevitably occurs. This is the strategy taken by many of the more formal politics-oriented groups in the Arab American community stage. However, those organizations struggle to maintain local power bases or connect with a majority of Arab Americans, particularly those who recently immigrated, speak Arabic as much as or more than English, or live outside of Michigan and/or those whose voices, opinions, and frameworks are most foreign to American politics and political conversations.[20]

But the other thing they can do is move politics away from the places where they face the highest risk of discursive misrecognition and into spaces that are more closed, more limited, and safer. That is, they can move politics into everyday, intracommunity spaces. These spaces provide environments where they can avoid, rearticulate, or reframe the demands discursive misrecognition sets. Politics moves away from the formal sphere and into the everyday; it is embedded in personal relationships, in "nonpolitical" spaces, and in movement contexts that share their own rules and principles about what is proper speech and action. By making this shift into other spaces of politics, Arab Americans chart out ways of being political actors that avoid, dismiss, or undermine the damage discursive misrecognition does to their political voices.

In this book, I look for the political in the everyday spaces that are a part of the collective community life of Arab Americans in New York. Some of these spaces have a tangible connection to more conventional notions of the political. Activists for Palestine, or pro–Arab Spring organizers, who organize demonstrations, rallies, boycotts, and social events, are clearly talking about an issue that is "political" by any definition. But rather than focusing on the claims they are making against the state (in many cases those claims are poorly articulated and not communicated) or their successes or failures in gaining concessions (those are few, far between, and often local), I analyze how these activist spaces frame different sorts of contestation and engagement and how differences in these framings influence how activist groups are received by outsiders and their possibilities for making change. This approach foregrounds the everyday of social movement practice, particularly with regard to how the identities of members in the groups are communicated and put to work in the process of the ongoing practices of social movement membership.

I also look for the political in the ordinary functioning of community groups, particularly those that provide social services to poor and recently immigrated Arabs. Most approaches to studying community groups look at them as loci of civic participation and study how civic participation is linked to political participation.[21] Other approaches examine how they help relate immigrants to the state and often deploy frameworks that depoliticize recipients of state services as mere clients rather than agentive political actors.[22] I focus on how, in Cordero-Guzmàn's terms, "immigrant organizations . . . explicitly incorporate cultural components, and a consciousness of ethnic or national origin identity, into their mission, practices, services and programs."[23] How do institutional, community-based organizations help members of immigrant communities explore how to live in their new home—a process that is necessarily political—while holding onto elements of older identities, which are inevitably transformed in the process? How do community organizations provide spaces for people to become engaged in public life and in contestation? How do people think together about politics in these social spaces? How are they influenced by power hierarchies and identities? What forms of contestation do they engage in, and what are the consequences of these contestations for the lives that participants construct for themselves?

The conventional view of Arab communities in the United States portrays Arab Americans as barely engaged in formal politics. But a more nuanced and complex notion of what politics entails lets us see something new: that Arab Americans are *differently* political, are profoundly engaged with political questions and the flows of political life, and, aware of that fact, engage in ways that don't match up neatly to expected forms. The everyday politics of Arab communities in New York is different from what many observers would expect from political life, but it is nonetheless vital for how Arab Americans come to understand themselves and their political capacities in American society.

Interpretive Ethnography: Centering Meaning Making in Everyday Spaces

My focus on the politics of the everyday, particularly how people engage in political discourses within everyday spaces, locates me as an interpretivist political scientist. Interpretive research prioritizes the ways that human beings invest meanings in the actions, words, and behaviors of others and aims to use the understanding of those meanings to make descriptive, causal, or normative claims about the world. Although interpretivists may not always agree on exactly how they conduct research and how they approach questions, they tend to have certain tendencies in common: they understand knowledge as historically situated and produced in power relationships, they are constructivist and believe that the world is intersubjective and socially produced, they reject individualist assumptions that assume people act independently of each other, at least in part, and they are interested in the way language and symbols work to create meaning and influence political life.[24]

Because my research was interpretive, I engaged closely and intimately with the people and communities I was studying in order to understand how the people in those spaces framed the issues they talked about. What did they mean when they used terms, made statements, organized activities? What were the values and associations they assigned to their actions? What do they understand about their actions, and what do others understand about them?

Particularly because I was investigating these questions in the everyday lives of Arabs in New York, I chose to use ethnography, a method that emphasizes the researcher's participation in everyday social spaces alongside the members of the community the scholar studies, trying to build an understanding of relevant elements of their lives from their own perspective. Ethnography as a method served a variety of purposes in my work. First, ethnography was well suited to the questions

I wanted to ask: it focused on the range of experiences (everyday life) I wanted to study, and it highlighted the conceptual material (people's meanings and understandings) that I wanted to understand. Although I also interviewed individuals in leadership positions of a broad range of community organizations and engaged in textual analysis of emails, newspapers, and organization documents, these were integrated into the broader framework of the ethnographic process. Ethnography was the best way that I could obtain the sort of data I wanted: to see how people talked about, interrogated, and contested political ideas in their daily lives.[25]

The second value of using ethnographic methods in this project has to do with the nature of the community I wanted to study and its current place in politics. Arab Americans are anxious about external observation because so much of that external observation is malicious in intent. Even observations that attempt to be friendly or supportive are often misguided, are awkward, or require the Arabs who are observed to engage in forced-speech situations or other unpleasant and undesired conversations. This is not a community that particularly wants to be studied, even though it lacks a choice in the matter. It is also a community that is capable of realizing that, frequently, the most truthful and honest answer to a question posed by an outsider may not be the best answer to give.

Appearing as a transient researcher without a foundation in the community would reveal only data at the margins. I was able to secure only a few interviews before I began my fieldwork and had deep community ties: one of those was openly hostile, and others contained some element of putting on public performances for an outsider. Therefore, part of the work of doing the research on this project involved putting myself in a position where members of the community would be willing to talk with me or to talk to others in front of me.

Once I began ethnographic fieldwork, I was granted access to a broader range of public and private moments of contestation and conversation. Frequently, I watched other participants in the spaces I was studying talk to outsiders, usually journalists, and, once the journalists had departed, turn back to the room and visibly change demeanor, moving from a performance for outsiders to one directed toward insiders. While I am an outsider in some significant and unchangeable ways, my position as a participant in the social spaces I was studying gave

Figure 1.1. The author poses with a Palestinian flag at a demonstration. I asked someone I knew to take the picture and joked, "At least my hair will look good when I'm on Campus Watch," a right-wing website that aimed to discredit academics who supported antiwar or pro-Palestinian positions.

me access to both registers of conversations. Ethnography was a productive method because, by being a participant in the processes I was documenting, I positioned myself to better gather data about the self-understandings and interpretations of the people I participated alongside and to map the space between my research subjects and myself.

The final reason for my reliance on ethnography relates to my normative commitments as a researcher, largely influenced by work in feminist research methods, but which are held by a large range of critical scholars. Rather than relying on an extractive notion of research, wherein the researchers enter a community, retrieve data, and then leave to use the data for their own purposes, I want to engage in a meaningful and reciprocal exchange with the communities I study, in whatever form makes sense for the particular project. In this case, I hope that the content of the research constitutes an intervention on behalf of the community, an attempt to change the way Arab Americans are thought and talked about, and heard or listened to, in American political life. I also wanted to contribute, in a concrete way, to projects important to the communities. My time spent as a volunteer within these organizations constituted such a contribution: I did necessary work, and I did it largely in ways directed by community needs and desires. Certainly, researchers collecting other sorts of data could make contributions like this and participate in these sorts of ways to get access to nonethnographic data. But combining these elements has a certain elegant efficiency to it.

My fieldwork stretched over approximately two years, beginning in September 2008 and continuing through October 2010, with initial forays beforehand and continued engagement afterward. Unlike much ethnographic fieldwork, which involves a sustained period of being constantly in the field for a defined period, wherein data are collected daily or almost daily before being processed, my fieldwork involved a constant shifting between being in and out of the field. For instance, a day of fieldwork frequently meant a few hours at the Arab American Association in Bay Ridge, teaching English to a class of immigrant women and chatting with the staff there, and then the commute back to my home in Kensington, a central Brooklyn neighborhood, where I would go to my local café and write up my field notes. Or it might mean a two-hour conference call in the evening with other members of Adalah-NY, one of the activist groups I studied, followed by a round of emails the next day about where to go after that conversation. Only rarely was fieldwork a "whole-day" experience, when I would spend four or six hours engaged in the field. The division also collapsed from the other direction: on a day when I was "out of the field," I would still receive emails from organizations I was studying, keep in touch with friends made during fieldwork on Facebook, and collect interesting bits of writing about Arab Americans or Arabs in New York that I found online or in print.

This was facilitated by the fact that I lived my daily life in the same city where I conducted my fieldwork. The center of Arab Bay Ridge is three miles from the apartment I lived in at the time, and the meetings of the activist group I participated in the most were about an hour subway ride, only slightly farther than my university campus. My experience as an ethnographer in Arab New York was made easier by the simple fact that I was, already, a New Yorker. I don't mean that in the literal sense that, as a resident of the city, I already had friends, contacts, a place to live, and a basic knowledge of geography, though these things were all true. Instead, what I already had was a large set of cultural understandings of what makes life in the city work: the codes of how to interact on city streets and public transportation, a set of common references to discuss with casual conversation partners, and a huge, preexisting set of connotative assumptions about neighborhoods, ethnic groups, and social institutions that could be used (and also were necessarily interrogated in the process).

In other words, I was already an insider to one of the social spheres that I shared with Arab New Yorkers. When my students and I sat around in Intermediate English, complaining about how expensive rent was, we were engaging in a traditional New York conversation, and I was a fully accredited participant. When activists in meetings I attended mentioned other activist groups, stores to demonstrate at, or communities to connect with, I understood their shorthand and was able to participate. (In fact, midway through my fieldwork with Adalah-NY, I ran into a member of the group whom I had worked with years before during my own activist days.) Knowing that I shared this common identity meant having to interrogate when we shared assumptions and when we didn't, but it provided a certain fluidity at the beginning of the process, which I was grateful for. While I agree with Bayard de Volo that "the researcher can never be fully familiar within what is considered her own culture," the initial familiarities I possessed did ease my way into the ethnographic process.[26]

However, my research has limits imposed by practical factors as well as by questions of identity. First, research for this project was conducted nearly entirely in English or "Arabish" (a fusion of the two languages). Many of the people I spoke with could code switch between an Arabic-inflected English and an English-inflected Arabic, depending on the audience. For instance, people spoke of going "to the *blad* [homeland]" for the summer and an employee of the Arab American Association made reference to "working at the *jama'iyya* [association]." Although I have a basic understanding of both spoken and written Arabic, my grasp of the language is far from fluent, which meant that large portions of conversations presented at everyday speed were lost to me and written texts required long, slow decoding, which was frequently not possible. I was therefore less of an audience for Arabic-only conversations, in which I could often get only the gist of what was being said, and my analysis is limited by this.

Second, this research does not cover all segments of Arab New York in equal depth. There are many, not necessarily contiguous Arab communities in the five boroughs, which are united by Arab ancestry but divided by religion, immigration status, language use, and geography. (To get from Bay Ridge, Brooklyn, to Astoria, Queens, the two largest Arab neighborhoods in the city, takes an hour and a half by subway, and more than half an hour by car.) Because my research methods required deep involvement in social spaces, I could not capture the entire patchwork in more than sketched-out terms. To be specific, my research focused on the hub of Bay Ridge, Brooklyn, which has the greatest density of people of Arab descent anywhere in New York City, and which also has older and more established social institutions than Astoria. My initial contacts in Bay Ridge were made through the Arab American Association, which was tremendously productive but showed me a different slice of the community than if my initial contacts had been with the Islamic Society of Bay Ridge or the Salam Lutheran Arabic Church, two other important social institutions in the neighborhood. My contacts were predominantly Muslims, who make up the majority of the more recent immigrant cohort, and from two sorts of backgrounds: either recent immigrants or the children of immigrants who may or may not have been born abroad but were raised in the United States.

When I chose to study Palestine activism, my connections were limited by the willingness of groups to engage with me and my ability to be connected, through personal networks, to those groups. Palestine activists are justifiably wary of political infiltrators, given the focus that pro-Israel activists put on understanding and documenting the tactics of their action in order to combat them. (For years, the best resource I could find on the timeline and history of one of the groups I was studying was their write-up by the Anti-Defamation League, a Jewish civil rights organization that monitors political activity opposed to Israeli policy.) In some cases, my background knowledge and experience in antiwar movements and, to a lesser extent, my prior experience studying social movements in Israel/Palestine helped provide me with a means to entry.[27] For others, I was stuck on the outside, observing more than participating and using data such as websites, social media feeds, federally gathered statistics, and observation without deep participation (such as attending and documenting a protest). While I provide a broad sketch of the institutions, demographics, and geography of the Arab communities of New York City as a whole, the deepest, and I hope most meaningful, parts of this research are focused on the areas where I was able to gain the deepest access.

I am also limited in that I stopped doing fieldwork in the late fall of 2010 and moved away from New York City in the summer of 2011, which meant I was no longer collecting data via participant observation. While all ethnographers leave the field eventually, the consequences are particularly important for this book because I was not in the field to collect data about the changes in Arab American community and political life after the Arab Uprisings of 2010–2011. My research on these questions was conducted at a distance, using more interviews and social media data than I used to study other questions. However, the same ethnographic sensibility drives my approach to that period, and I believe that the frameworks developed in my ethnographic engagement apply to this newer period. I address these methodological questions in the chapter where I use these data.

Plan of the Book

I have organized the remainder of the book into three main sections, which present different angles on the Arab communities in New York, their everyday lives, and their relationships to politics. In the first section, "Everyday Lives," I include this introductory chapter and the second chapter, a detailed geography of the Arab communities of New York City. I present a demographic analysis of the population of Arab descent within New York's five boroughs, working from the statistical data produced by the American Community Survey. Following this quantitative description, I lay out a more material geography of Arab New York, focusing on the neighborhoods where populations and community organizations are centered. In this chapter, I also introduce the three organizations that made up my field sites: the Arab American Association of New York, Adalah-NY: The New York Campaign for the Boycott of Israel, and Al-Awda NY: The Palestine Right to Return

Coalition. In addition to serving as a reference for the rest of the book, this chapter also records a moment in Arab New York's history that has not yet been documented in the research into US Arab communities, so that those who are interested in Arab New York can have a background picture to measure changes or variations against their own experiences, observations, or research.

The second section, "Everyday Contestations," focuses on the ways that individuals engage in micropolitical contestations in their everyday lives, particularly through the lens of civic engagement in Arab- or Muslim-identified institutions. The third chapter explores how community educational institutions serve as focal points for the making of a collective Arab identity, which is a necessary precursor to other forms of political engagement. Because educational spaces are designed to create exchanges between individuals and require them to explicitly explain and demonstrate their thoughts and feelings, they are able to present ideas of what they share in common and how they differentiate themselves from the non-Arabs they share their neighborhood and city with. In addition, educational spaces provide the opportunity to engage with other Arabs in an environment of minimal surveillance by non-Arabs, which helps to avoid issues of discursive misrecognition, and in the context of a community-based organization, which can be critical to immigrant political incorporation. By focusing on how the adult women in an English as a second language class and the elementary-school-aged children in a summer camp program used language and signs to define themselves and developed new Arab identities that were specific to diaspora, I explore the way that these community spaces make possible forms of political engagement and action.

The fourth chapter explores the role of young Arab women, particularly high school and college students, as leaders in Muslim and Arab community organizing. These young women work under a double burden of observation and surveillance from other members of the Arab community as well as from non-Arab interlocutors, both of whom have a long list of rhetorical demands that they make of young women who appear in public. While these young women are the backbone of much community organizing, they must constantly manage expectations from both of these groups of interlocutors—who are often asking for irreconcilable things. In this chapter, I profile young women active in the community and explore the way that they position themselves dialogically against their interlocutors in order to manage these competing demands for justification.

The last section, "Everyday Identities," examines how Arab identities are put to work in the quotidian practices of social movements—that is, how the everyday is connected to the formally political. The fifth chapter turns to the largest and most ongoing form of political engagement for most people of Arab descent in New York: activism in support of Palestine. I analyze two very different organizations, showing how the deep diversity of people of Arab descent in New York helps produce very different forms of political engagement around Palestinian liberation. Each of these groups deploys a different set of identity roles, both among different Arabs and between Arab and non-Arab members, which allow them access to different potential members, different types of language and discourse, and different interlocutors.

The sixth chapter moves from investigating the ongoing mobilization in support of Palestine to examining activism promoting the wave of revolutions and regime changes of 2010–2011. Both Arab Americans who had previously been engaged in other forms of community and political organizing and others who had previously not been so engaged formed new coalitions and organizations to support the Egyptian and Yemeni revolutionaries in their advocacy for new, more democratic governance in their countries. These organizations were built using the tools that had previously been employed for community organizing and activism for Palestine, but required activating new arguments to justify these actions, as well as new identities, such as national identities, that had previously been secondary to religious or panethnic identities.

In the conclusion, I return to the question of why everyday politics is so important for the study of politics in general and demonstrate its centrality to the research in this book. In addition, I turn to the political moment in which this book is being finished, the early days of Donald J. Trump's presidential administration, and ask how the position of Arab Americans in American political life is shifting, as politics changes and moves on.

2

Mapping Arab New York

Complexity and Community

As discussed in chapter 1, the Arab community in the United States is incredibly diverse. Some of this diversity results from the range of people who call themselves or are called Arab, in terms of nationality, religion, and other identities. Another major factor in the diversity of Arab Americans is the variety of historical moments and legal regimes under which Arabs have immigrated to the United States. People from the Arab world have been immigrating to the country since the mid-nineteenth century, with the first major wave of migration occurring between the 1880s and the 1920s. In 1924, the Immigration Act implemented strict entry quotas designed to restrict immigrants from Southern and Eastern Europe and East Asia; as a not-quite-intended consequence, there was a near total cessation of immigration from the Middle East as well. Another wave of Arab immigration began in the late 1960s, when the 1965 lifting of quota restrictions coincided with the 1967 war between Israel and its neighbors, displacing many Arabs and convincing both those displaced and others to seek safety and success elsewhere. The flows from the Arab world to the United States have continued, including a mix of economic migration, family reunification, student migration, and refugee resettlement.

These two waves of migration were very different. Those who came during the first wave were largely Christian migrants from the Ottoman province of Syria, many from what is now Lebanon, and others from what is now Syria. Contemporary migrants come from a broad range of Arab countries, particularly Egypt, Palestine, Iraq, and Yemen, in addition to Syria and Lebanon, and are predominantly Muslim. For example, according to the 2012 Global Religious Landscape study by the Pew Research Center, 3 percent of Christian authorized immigrants to the United States but 31 percent of Muslim authorized immigrants have their origins in the Middle East or North Africa. While there are about six times as many Christian immigrants as Muslim in the United States, that still suggests more Muslims than Christians immigrate from the Middle East. The early migrants came mostly as peddlers and unskilled laborers; although unskilled workers do still immigrate to the United States from Arab countries, many more are professionals who arrive with either human or economic capital.[1]

However, New York City has been integral to both waves of migration. New York was the "mother colony" of Arab migration to the United States during the first wave. A vibrant Little Syria flourished in what is now the financial district of Manhattan, eventually being displaced to Downtown Brooklyn along Atlantic Avenue. Arabs arriving from the Middle East passed through New York en route to either other urban centers or to work as door-to-door peddlers. Some of the infrastructure created by these first-wave Arab migrants persists today: the Maronite and Antiochian Orthodox cathedrals built for these communities in Brooklyn Heights are still the major centers of worship for the region, and Sahadi's, one of the original dry goods stores supplying goods to peddlers, has become an upscale spice and food shop in Boerum Hill. At present, the New York metropolitan area is home to the third largest community of people of Arab descent in the United States, after Los Angeles and Detroit (and followed by Chicago and Washington, DC).

The purpose of this chapter is to provide the reader with a series of different analytical lenses for thinking about what it means to talk about Arab New York, as I do in this book. As a blanket term, it refers to a tremendously diverse group of people, united only by living within the boundaries of New York City and at least partial ancestry in the Arabic-speaking countries of the Middle East and North Africa. People of Arab descent in New York may be Christian, Muslim, or Jewish; may be recent immigrants, have immigrated decades ago, or be part of the second, third, or fourth generation; may live closely connected to their extended families or may have left that family in Detroit, Al-Bireh, or Los Angeles; may speak Arabic, English, or another language in their daily life.

Fundamentally, there are two conceptual ways to understand what makes up an Arab American community. On the one hand, the Arab American community of a place is made up of all community residents who have Arab ancestry. This is the definition used by organizations like the Arab American Institute in producing demographic profiles of Arab Americans and certainly has the advantage of being all-encompassing. However, it lacks nuance. Individuals can have Arab ancestry, but that identity can be largely unimportant to them—perhaps a few family traditions of food or music, but nothing that influences how they think about themselves or their place in society. For others, their identity as Arabs might be important, but they might lack a meaningful community of other Arabs, particularly in face-to-face contexts, and find their most important communal experiences in religious, place-based, professional, or other communities. Arab-identified people might also choose to shun the community of other Arabs, particularly in instances where they disagree with prevailing norms and practices in those communities. Public actors will often claim to represent all of these people—who have not, in the normal course of things, had the chance to weigh in on how they are represented. At the same time, scholars who want to research the Arab community have to figure out how to define such a community. But given the diversity of Arabs and the multifarious ways that people can belong or fail to belong to an Arab community, this seems to be a project that is destined to fail.

To set the stage for this work while trying to avoid the desire to strictly codify one idea of *the* Arab community of New York, this chapter provides three lenses through which to think about what constitutes Arab New York. The first is demographic and is based entirely on identification as having an Arab ancestry on the American Community Survey, annually conducted by the US Census Bureau and the most consistent national-level statistical product that allows people to identify as Arab. The ACS is a tremendously flawed instrument for talking about people of Arab descent, as I will discuss, but this sort of high-level statistical work is the best way to capture all people who identify any Arab ancestry, for taking the broadest view of who might identify as part of an Arab community and getting a sense of what that means at a citywide scale.

The second lens is through the idea of "Arab neighborhoods." There are three neighborhoods in New York City that can be labeled as Arab, for reasons connected to their history, the location of Arab-identified institutions, and the presence of a large number of Arab-identified people. Bay Ridge and Atlantic Avenue in Brooklyn and Astoria in Queens have different ethnic makeups, levels of community institutionalization, and social characteristics. (They are also all diverse; none of them are exclusively or even majority Arab.) Neighborhoods are an important place where people find community. A neighborhood with a high concentration of coethnics can be the location where the idea of an ethnic community goes from abstract to concrete, personified in personal and institutional connections. A large portion of my research focused on Bay Ridge in particular, making a neighborhood-based analysis essential to understanding the material. To support that, I introduce not only Bay Ridge but also Astoria and Atlantic Avenue as a way of painting a broad picture of New York's Arab communities at the neighborhood level.

The third lens I present is community organizations. In New York, like in other American cities, community-based organizations are a major driver of ethnic community, alongside religious institutions, schools, and social movement activities. I chose to use organizations as my entry point into Arab New York, with a particular focus on both service organizations and activist groups. All of these groups had an Arab identity, and people who chose to participate in their activities had to make an active decision to participate in an Arab group—to join an Arab community of practice. (Not all of those people were themselves Arab, a point that I discuss throughout.) This section sketches the broad landscape of community organizations of different types and then focuses in on the particular organizations I worked with for this research. By doing so, it provides a description of the places in New York where an idea of Arab community is practiced as a way of opening up the analysis.

Different readers may have different approaches to this chapter. Those who have absolutely no interest in reading statistics may want to skim over the demographic section; the key takeaway is that people of Arab descent in New York are diverse in terms of national origin, immigration status, language use, and socioeconomic status and that different national origin groups have different histories and statuses. Those already familiar with the neighborhoods of New York, particularly Bay Ridge in the 2010s, may choose to skim the section on neighborhood geography. The final section, on community organizations, will most certainly be helpful for introducing the organizations where I carried out fieldwork, and readers might find it useful to refer back to at later points if they find themselves confused about those organizations mentioned in later chapters. In total, this chapter preserves for posterity the

Arab New York(s) in which I worked in the early 2010s and provides future researchers and community workers with some background from which to approach my conclusions and compare their own observations and insights about Arab communities in this city and others.

Arab New York in Numbers

Gathering good quantitative data about people of Arab descent in the United States is notoriously difficult. There is no ongoing demographic research specifically focused on understanding where Arab Americans live, what their social conditions are, or where they are from. The US Census Bureau classifies them as white, thereby hiding them within the rest of the population. Nearly all researchers rely on the bureau's annual American Community Survey (ACS), which follows appropriate social science protocols for a national-level survey and produces comparable data from year to year. However, there are serious problems with the ACS data for quantifying Arab Americans.

First, because of small sample sizes for Arab communities in the ACS, margins of error for these populations can reach 50 percent or higher in some places, though my casual glance through the ACS data used below suggests that it is more often between 15 and 30 percent. Most national-level Arab American organizations believe very strongly that there is a major undercount in how many people of Arab descent are in the United States. The Arab American Institute (AAI), a national organization that dedicates significant energy to providing a demographic picture of the national Arab American community, identifies four causes of this undercount in its literature: "the placement of and limit of the ancestry question (as distinct from race and ethnicity); the effect of the sample methodology on small, unevenly distributed ethnic groups; high levels of out-marriage among the third and fourth generations; and distrust/misunderstanding of government surveys among recent immigrants."[2] I would argue that these four causes are very different in their possible effects; people who do not list an Arab ancestry because of out-marriage are unlikely to be active members of an Arab community of practice, for instance. However, this does mean that the best, most consistent data sources we can get on Arab Americans are inevitably undercounting them, and we do not know precisely *how* they undercount them.

Other researchers have conducted their own high-quality quantitative surveys that aim to specifically sample the Arab-identified population in particular locations or contexts.[3] I did not undertake such a study in New York City. While a worthwhile project in the abstract, it would have required resources beyond my capacity to organize. Instead, I chose to follow AAI's practice in using the ACS statistics to provide a profile of people of Arab descent in New York, while being humble about the fact that we know these numbers to be flawed.

During the time of my research in 2010 and 2011, the ACS estimated that there were around 1.9 million people of Arab descent in the United States; the AAI estimated that the number was closer to 3.6 million.[4] Nationally, a plurality of people of Arab descent identify as Lebanese (27 percent), followed by Egyptians (11 percent), Syrians (8 percent), Palestinians (5 percent), Iraqis (5 percent), and a number of smaller groups. However, 15 percent of those surveyed by the ACS identify themselves solely as Arab/Arabic, which obscures their national origins. At least for the foreign-born population that identifies as Arab/Arabic, 14.8 percent were born in the countries of North Africa (mostly Egypt and Morocco), 12.7 percent in Jordan, 12.5 percent in Iraq, 11 percent in Yemen, and 6 percent in Israel. It is likely that many of those born in Jordan as well as a majority of those born in Israel have Palestinian roots.[5]

New York State has approximately 159,000 residents of Arab descent, the third largest population of people of Arab descent nationally. In New York State as a whole, the entire population of Arab descent is 21 percent Lebanese, 18 percent Egyptian, 11 percent Syrian, 8 percent Moroccan, and 4 percent each Palestinian and Jordanian. Of Arab residents of New York State, 17 percent identify as Arab/Arabic; 34 percent of those who were born abroad were born in Yemen, 10 percent in Jordan, 7.5 percent in Saudi Arabia, and 5 percent in Israel.

New York City is the demographic center of the state's Arab population. For instance, the five counties with the largest Arab populations are Kings (Brooklyn), Queens, New York (Manhattan), Westchester (the first suburban county north of the city), and Richmond (Staten Island). Of the 159,000 people of Arab descent the ACS counts in New York State, over 94,000 live in the five boroughs of New York. The community is concentrated in Brooklyn and Queens (approximately 40,000 in Brooklyn and over 20,000 in Queens), with substantial numbers also

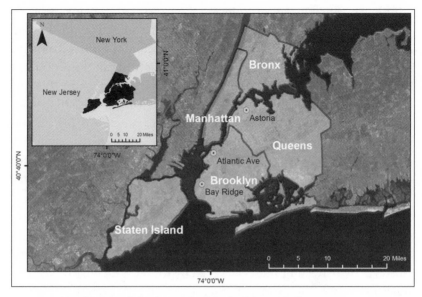

Figure 2.1. New York City's five boroughs. Map by Edmar Miglhorance.

living in the other boroughs; while Staten Island only has around 9,000 people of Arab descent, they constitute about 2 percent of the borough's population, more than the percentage they represent in the much more populous (for both Arabs and non-Arabs) Brooklyn.

Of the Arab-identified population in New York City, 47 percent were born in the United States, while 53 percent were born abroad. Of those born abroad, 60 percent have become naturalized citizens. Of those born abroad, 58 percent are men, and 60 percent of those who have become naturalized citizens are male as well. Of the foreign-born population, 61 percent entered before 2000, 33.2 percent entered between 2000 and 2009, and 5.5 percent entered after 2010. The foreign-born population is from a mix of countries, with the most common being Egypt (26 percent), Yemen (16 percent), Morocco (13 percent), Lebanon (9 percent), Syria (5 percent), Jordan (4 percent), and Israel (3 percent). Compared to the national Arab American population, New York's is more heavily immigrant (53 percent in NYC vs. 43 percent nationwide), and its foreign-born population is both slightly more heavily naturalized (60 percent in NYC vs. 57 percent nationwide) and more likely to be North African (41 percent born in Africa in NYC vs. 29 percent nationwide).

The majority of Arabs in New York City (65.8 percent) live in family households, meaning that two or more people related by birth, marriage, or adoption live together; 52.9 percent of the Arab population lives in households with a married couple, and only 5.6 percent of family households are headed by women. Nearly 54 percent of the population over fifteen is married, and nearly 37 percent are never married, while only 4.8 percent are divorced. The average family size is 4.07 individuals, while the average household size (including nonfamily households) is 3.18 individuals. Over 30 percent of the population is seventeen or younger. These are all roughly consistent with the nationwide Arab population, although New Yorkers are slightly less likely to be divorced (7.1 percent of the nationwide population) and have slightly larger family sizes (3.73 people nationwide).

Arabs in New York are well educated in general. Over 30 percent have a bachelor's degree and 17 percent have a graduate or professional degree (compared to 19.9 percent of New Yorkers with a bachelor's degree and 13.8 percent with a graduate or professional degree). Men and women have similar levels of education, with 49 percent of men and 45 percent of women having a bachelor's degree or higher. Because of this high level of education, 41.6 percent of all Arabs in New York work in management or professional positions, 32.5 percent in sales or office jobs, and 11.9 percent in service jobs. Women are much more heavily represented in management or professional jobs (54.5 percent of working women have management or professional jobs, as opposed to 36.6 percent of men). However, only slightly more than 40 percent of women are in the labor force, as opposed to 59.3 percent of women in the population as a whole. This suggests that working-class and lower income families are more likely to be single-breadwinner households than those where the adults have professional or managerial jobs. This is also reflected in income figures: the median household income is $51,400, while the mean is $87,164. (Again reflecting the gender imbalance in career trajectory, women make more than men on average: among full-time, year-round workers, women make over $53,000 a year, while men make over $47,000.) The demographics for Arabs in New York are roughly comparable to the Arab American population as a whole ($52,447 median, $81,176 mean) and slightly higher than the general population of New York City ($50,711 median, $79,740 mean).

However, the high incomes and educational success of a significant percentage of the Arab-descended population of New York City does not mean that all Arabs in the city are economically prosperous. Nearly 22 percent of families and 24 percent of individuals live below the poverty line. In particular, 32 percent of all Arab children in New York live in poverty. Nearly 41 percent receive their health insurance through a public program, such as Medicaid or Medicare, rather than through their employers or private purchase, and 13.6 percent receive SNAP (food stamp) benefits.[6] A particularly high percentage of Arab families in Brooklyn are recipients of benefits: 19.9 percent of Arab families in Brooklyn receive SNAP benefits, compared to 12.0 percent in Queens, and 49 percent of Brooklyn families have public health insurance, as opposed to 42 percent in Queens.[7] This is the case despite the facts that the poverty rates in Brooklyn and Queens are fairly close (24.2 percent in Brooklyn, 23.0 percent in Queens) and that the child poverty rate is even higher in Queens (39.0 percent as opposed to 34.8 percent in Brooklyn). This gap probably reflects the greater institutionalization and strength of Arab community organizations in Brooklyn, which provide a means of connecting Arab families to government services.

Despite the fact that a large proportion of Arab Americans in New York were born in the United States, Arabic is a frequently used language within the community. Only 29.2 percent of Arab households speak only English at home, and 70.8 percent speak a language other than English, usually Arabic (although some speak French or Spanish, sometimes because of migration to Spanish- or French-speaking countries, sometimes because of the class distribution of European languages in Arab countries). However, of adults who speak another language at home, only 27.6 percent speak English "less than very well," which means that a large percentage of people of Arab descent are functionally multilingual, at least for everyday encounters in both languages. This contrasts with the Arab population in the United States as a whole, where 42.4 percent of Arab households speak only English at home, and 21.1 percent of those who speak another language lack high English proficiency.

The demographics presented thus far apply to all individuals and families of Arab descent in New York City. However, as we saw when comparing the Arab populations of Brooklyn and Queens, not all Arab people, families, or communities are the same. One of the easiest ways to see this is to disaggregate the Arab community into national origin groups. Of the Arab population of New York City, 23 percent identify themselves as Egyptian, 20 percent as Arab/Arabic, 15 percent as Lebanese, 11.9 percent as Moroccan, 8.5 percent as Yemeni, 4.5 percent as Palestinian, 2 percent as Algerian, and less than 2 percent each as Iraqi or Jordanian. The 20 percent who identify as Arab/Arabic are 57 percent foreign-born and 43 percent native-born; of the foreign-born, a plurality (35 percent) were born in Yemen. Several of the other largest countries of birth (Jordan, 9 percent; Egypt, 7.6 percent; Israel, 3.4 percent; Syria, 2.5 percent) have substantial Palestinian populations, which suggests that another significant proportion of the Arab/Arabic population may have Palestinian ancestry but either may be unwilling to put "Palestinian" on an official form or do not substantively identify as Palestinian.

Each community has a particular demographic profile, although again there is significant diversity within national origin communities. The Syrian community, for instance, has the highest proportion of native-born US citizens (71.7 percent), and 63 percent of foreign-born Syrians have gained US citizenship. Also, 60 percent speak English at home, and fewer than 16 percent speak English less than very well. Nearly 37 percent of Syrian households make less than $50,000, while nearly 46 percent make more than $75,000 and 34 percent make more than $100,000. In total, 12.8 percent of Syrian individuals, 10.4 percent of Syrian families, and 12.8 percent of Syrian children live in poverty in New York. The Lebanese community is also majority US-born (56 percent), highly naturalized (60.2 percent), and slightly less English speaking (47.1 percent speak English at home, 10.4 percent speak an Indo-European language other than Spanish, likely French, and 20.8 percent speak English less than very well). They also have a substantial population who is economically well-off; while nearly 42 percent make less than $50,000, 29.9 percent make more than $100,000, and only 7.5 percent of families, 10.4 percent of individuals, and 10.4 percent of children live in poverty. It seems possible that a good proportion of the Syrian and Lebanese population in New York City consists of long-assimilated descendants of Lebanese and Syrian immigrants from the first wave of Arab immigration to the United States, while others are more recent arrivals or their descendants, particularly those leaving because of the Lebanese Civil War and related conflicts in both countries.

Egyptians, the largest community, present a different picture. Of Egyptians in New York, 62 percent were born abroad, and 74 percent of those immigrated after 2000. Only 25.5 percent speak English at home. However, they are generally highly educated; 93 percent have at least a high school diploma and 57 percent have at least a bachelor's degree. (However, 30 percent speak English less than very well, implying that many received their education in Arabic and speak only rudimentary English.) There are significant numbers of Egyptians at both ends of the economic spectrum: 45.4 percent make less than $50,000, but 25.9 percent make more than $100,000. Over 19 percent of Egyptian individuals, 18 percent of Egyptian families, and a full 28 percent of Egyptian children in New York live below the poverty line. Nearly 44 percent of the Egyptians in New York work in management or professional positions, and significant numbers also work in sales/office (22 percent) and service jobs (13.6 percent). So the Egyptian community includes both many immigrants with high human and economic capital and those who are struggling.

The demographic profile of Yemenis is very different. Of Yemenis, 63 percent were born abroad. They have the lowest level of educational attainment of all Arab communities: only 62 percent have a high school degree, and under 14 percent have a bachelor's degree. Only 11.2 percent speak English at home, and 55.4 percent of those who speak another language do not speak English very well. This is unsurprising, given that Yemen is the only country in the Arab world designated by the United Nations as a least developed country (ranked 168 of 188 in the world in 2016) and has a relatively high level of illiteracy (77 percent of Yemeni men and 41 percent of Yemeni women are literate) and low educational attainment (average of slightly more than four years of education on average for men and just under two years for women). Yemenis also have the smallest percentage of women in the workforce, at only 22.8 percent (compared to 48.7 percent for Egyptians, for instance, or 70.5 percent for Iraqis), which also may be connected to women's poor educational attainment. Of Yemeni households, 71 percent make less than $50,000, and only 7.2 percent make more than $100,000. A large majority of Yemenis (71.6 percent) work in sales or office positions. Qualitatively, many run bodegas, neighborhood convenience stores. Nearly 37 percent of Yemeni individuals, 35 percent of Yemeni families, and a stunning 50.2 percent of Yemeni children live in poverty. However, Yemeni families receive very little support from the US government (only 6.7 percent of Yemeni families receive SNAP benefits), likely in part because they are recently immigrated and not naturalized and in part because they are unable to access services due to linguistic limits. So while Egyptians are largely economically successful and highly educated, Yemenis are poor and struggling to make ends meet, particularly families with children.

Palestinians are another major community in my research, although they are not well numerically represented in the ACS data set. This may be because Palestinians are more poorly captured by the ACS than other Arab Americans or particularly likely to choose an identifier other than "Palestinian" because of stigmas against Palestinians in the United States, or because Palestinians are more worried than other Arabs about government action against them. But based on those who identified as Palestinian in this data set, a slight majority were born in the United States (just under 55 percent). Most of the foreign-born are recent immigrants (80.4 percent since 2000), and nearly 65 percent of foreign-born Palestinians now hold US citizenship. Palestinians are generally well educated (71.5 percent with a high school diploma, 29.9 percent with at least a bachelor's degree). Only 21 percent speak English at home, and only 36 percent speak English less than very well; 48.5 percent make under $50,000, and 22.7 percent make more than $100,000. Around 21 to 22 percent of Palestinian individuals, families, and children live in poverty. Just barely under half of Palestinians work in sales or office positions; like Yemenis, many own or run bodegas. The profile of Palestinians more closely resembles that of Egyptians than those of other groups.

Moroccans, the last major national origin group, occupy a place somewhere between Palestinians and Yemenis in social and demographic characteristics. Of Moroccans, 63 percent were born abroad but 37.6 percent arrived before 2000, with 62.4 percent arriving after, making them more like Yemenis (62.8 percent of whom arrived after 2000) than other groups in terms of immigrant profile. But 30 percent of Moroccan households speak English, 17.2 percent speak a non-Spanish Indo-European language (likely French, the language of the educated elite in Morocco), and 30 percent of those who do not speak English at home speak English less than very well, more like the Lebanese. Nearly

84 percent have high school diplomas and 27.2 percent have bachelor's degrees, and their occupations are remarkably evenly split among management and professional positions (33.3 percent), service positions (22.3 percent), production and transportation positions (20.4 percent), and sales and office positions (20.3 percent), giving them much less sectorial concentration than other Arab communities. Just under 53 percent make less than $50,000, putting them slightly under the median income for all Arabs in the city, and only 17.5 percent make more than $100,000, again suggesting a wide dispersal of incomes that average out near the mean. Poverty is also significant but not epidemic among Moroccans, with 19.8 percent of individuals, 18.6 percent of families, and 19.8 percent of children living in poverty.

Different nationality communities are distributed differently across the five boroughs. Based on an analysis of Yemenis, Egyptians, Lebanese, Moroccans, Palestinians, Syrians, and those who responded "Arab/ Arabic" and who live in Brooklyn, Queens, Manhattan, or Staten Island, the largest Yemeni, Palestinian, Lebanese, and Syrian populations are in Brooklyn, while the largest Egyptian and Moroccan populations are in Queens. Arabs in Queens, of all nationalities, are the most likely to be immigrants: only in Queens are immigrant Lebanese a majority of Lebanese residents (56.1 percent, as opposed to between 36 and 44 percent in the other boroughs), and Egyptians and Arab/Arabic responders also show around 10 percent more immigrants than in Brooklyn or elsewhere. Arabic speakers are also unequally distributed among the boroughs. In Brooklyn, Syrians are the only Arab nationality where a majority speak English at home, while 47.3 percent of Lebanese do; for other nationalities, the percentages range from 8.8 percent for Yemenis to 28.3 percent for Moroccans. Staten Island is similar, where 47 percent of Lebanese and 79 percent of Syrians speak English at home, but only 12.8 percent of Egyptians and 22.4 percent of Arab/Arabic respondents do. In Queens, no Arab nationality group has a higher than 31 percent rate of speaking English at home, whereas in Manhattan only "Arab/ Arabic" respondents have a lower than 45 percent rate of speaking English at home (at 19.8 percent). So Queens has a majority Arabic-speaking Arab population, Brooklyn and Staten Island have both Anglophone and Arabic-speaking populations, and Manhattan is majority Anglophone. In every community in every borough, the mean income is higher than the median income (meaning there are some very high income outliers), and incomes in Manhattan are significantly higher than those in any other borough, followed by Staten Island. Brooklyn and Queens are roughly equivalent for all groups.

These statistics reflect the Arab-descended population of New York City when I was conducting my research. In the time between then and the publication of this book, not much has changed. Based on the 2015 ACS five-year survey, there are approximately the same number of Arab-identified people living in the five boroughs as there were during my research (94,130). Similar to before, 44 percent (a plurality) live in Brooklyn, 21 percent in Queens, 15 percent in Manhattan, 11 percent in Staten Island, and 8 percent in the Bronx. There has been some shift in terms of national origin proportions. In all, 23 percent identify as Egyptian, 16 percent as Arab/Arabic, 12 percent as Lebanese, 11 percent as Syrian, 11 percent as Yemeni, 8.7 percent as Moroccan, 4.4 percent as Palestinian, and 1.5 percent as Jordanian. Fifty percent are foreign-born—only Manhattan has substantially less than 50 percent foreign-born Arabs. Of those born abroad, 30 percent are Egyptian, 18 percent are Yemeni, 9.7 percent are Moroccan, 8.2 percent are Syrian, and 7.6 percent are Lebanese (3 percent each were born in Jordan and Israel, which may mean that a decent number of those people identify as Palestinian, as may some born in Lebanon, Syria, and Egypt). Of the foreign-born who identified as "Arab/Arabic," 32 percent were born in Yemen, 16 percent in Egypt, 7.5 percent in Syria, 5.4 percent in Israel, 5.6 percent in Jordan (suggesting they may be of Palestinian origin), and 5.9 percent in Morocco. Of the population, 29 percent speak English at home and 71 percent speak another language, while 28 percent speak English less than very well. The median income is similar ($55,381) and very close to the citywide mean ($53,373).

It's probably not worth reading too much into any variations in these numbers, given the known flaws with the ACS and the minor changes, most of which would not pass a test of statistical significance. However, I do want to remark on two minor changes, which may reflect an underlying transformation. First, 37 percent of the Syrian-identified population is now foreign-born, up from 28 percent during my research. To me, this suggests a new wave of arrivals of Syrians coming to the United States as refugees, family reunification migrants, or even students, fleeing the

Syrian conflict and adding a new dimension to a part of the community that was mostly US-born and long settled. Second, there are now enough Arabs in the Bronx to produce estimates about them. The Bronx is home to 8 percent of the Arab population of New York, and over 30 percent of them identified as Yemeni and another 26 percent as "Arab." (Given that 51 percent of the foreign-born Arabs in the Bronx were born in Yemen, it's safe to assume that many of that 26 percent of "Arab" identifiers are Yemeni.) In fact, at least a quarter of all Yemenis in New York live in the Bronx now. The demographics of Arab New York are constantly shifting and provide a particular window onto understanding how the diverse people who share Arab ancestry can gather and group themselves into different lived communities in multiple ways over time, as these shifts arise.

Neighborhood Geography

Ethnic neighborhoods have been a central consideration for scholars of immigration since the early twentieth century and are an enduring feature of journalistic and public attention to immigrant communities. But why, particularly, should we think of ethnic neighborhoods as important? As discussed above, people of a given ethnicity (or panethnicity) are tremendously diverse. Are those who live in ethnic neighborhoods any more worthy of study or any more politically interesting than their coethnics who live elsewhere?

This question seems particularly pertinent in New York City, where there are no neighborhoods that are majority Arab. In fact, there are very few places in the city with a truly high concentration of people of Arab descent. The only zip code in Brooklyn where more than 10 percent of the population identify as having Arab ancestry is 11209, which belongs to Bay Ridge, a neighborhood at the foot of the Verrazano-Narrows Bridge where 12.8 percent of the population identify as Arab. Plenty of New York neighborhoods have substantial populations of a single racial or panethnic group: Corona, Queens, is 72.6 percent Latino, and East Flatbush, Brooklyn, is 90.2 percent black. Sunset Park, just to Bay Ridge's northeast, is 38.8 percent Latino and 38.1 percent Chinese, in addition to having 3.1 percent Arab residents. However, as Logan and colleagues show in their examination of immigrant enclaves and ethnic communities in New York and Los Angeles, most ethnic neighborhoods have significant proportions of members of other groups, with concentrations of coethnics ranging "from a low value of 4.3 percent Filipino in Filipino suburban neighborhoods to a high of around 30 percent in Afro-Caribbean, Dominican, and Chinese city neighborhoods."[8]

Examining New York City by zip code suggests that only in a corner of southwest Brooklyn (Bay Ridge and the surrounding neighborhoods) is there a concentration of Arab-identifying people above 4 percent of the population. There are twenty-three zip codes across the city where more than 2 percent of the population is Arab identified, twice the proportion of Arabs in the total population of the city. Four of those zip codes are on Staten Island, eight in Brooklyn, and eight in Queens.

But ethnic concentration is only one part of the story of why ethnic neighborhoods might matter. In terms of city politics, in places where enough members of an ethnic group have US citizenship and are voters, they can constitute a meaningful voting bloc and influence the composition of city government. (It's not surprising that the city council members representing Harlem and Bedford-Stuyvesant are both black, that the representatives of Manhattan's Chinatown and Flushing, an Asian-majority neighborhood in Queens, are both Chinese immigrants, and that the representative for East Harlem is Puerto Rican and the representative of Sunset Park is Mexican.) Even where the percentage of voters is not high enough to ensure descriptive representation, a group might still represent a bloc to be courted. Neighborhoods with high concentrations of coethnics can also become home to a concentration of ethnic businesses, providing an economic sphere that allows people to obtain goods and services that are important to maintaining performances of their identity, such as ethnic or religious clothing, foods not available in mainstream American grocers, newspapers in their mother tongue, or culturally sensitive services like hairdressers for women who cover their hair. These businesses often provide first work opportunities for new immigrants without English skills as well.

Ethnic neighborhoods are also a fertile location for community organizations that specifically bring together members of an ethnic group. For new immigrants, being able to receive social services in their first language and getting an introduction to their new country through others who have immigrated from similar contexts are major benefits. Others may seek out culturally competent services or make a guess that a group of coethnics might be less likely to be discriminatory. Social service and community organizations in ethnic neighborhoods serve these functions of providing needed services to coethnics and are often located in neighborhoods where a large percentage of coethnics live. (Those who live outside the neighborhoods will travel to have their needs met.)

Although the possibility of power within local politics and the availability of ethnic goods, services, and organizations are some of the reasons why ethnic neighborhoods matter for studying ethnic groups, they are particularly important when working from an everyday politics perspective. Ethnic neighborhoods create space for coethnics to form meaningful community through daily practice. Public sphere places including playgrounds, houses of worship, school yards, public libraries, restaurants, and coffee shops all allow for the formation of community and, in places with a high percentage of coethnics, provide opportunities for an ethnic community to be formed out of a mass of people who share a background. The geographic concentration of people who might belong to such a community, coupled with public (and private) sphere spaces that allow for the practices that build the community, produces what I referred to in the first chapter as a community in practice, a group of people who understand themselves as connected to others who are like them in meaningful ways (and possibly unlike them in some other ways) and who act and behave in ways that assume that community and work to sustain it. While communities in practice can and do arise without a geographical locus, sharing the daily territory of a neighborhood certainly facilitates its formation.

Bay Ridge, a working-class neighborhood at Brooklyn's western edge, not only has the highest concentration of Arabs in the city but is also the core of *institutionalized* Arab New York. Not only do people of Arab origin live there, but community organizations, businesses, churches, and mosques oriented toward them have taken root, radiating out from the central strip of Fifth Avenue between Sixty-Eighth and Seventy-Second streets.

When I began my fieldwork, I mapped the storefronts along this strip, trying to quantify how this concentration worked. In the summer of 2009, only two stores on the two blocks before Sixty-Seventh and Sixty-Eighth were marked as Arab or as catering to an Arab community.

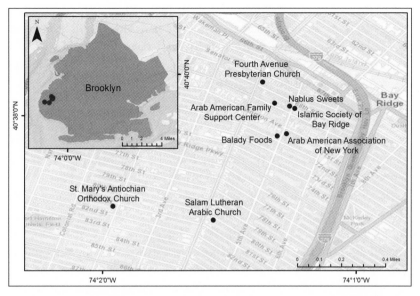

Figure 2.2. Bay Ridge, Brooklyn, has the densest population of Arab ancestry in New York City. In addition, the neighborhood has a high level of institutionalization, including the main office of the Arab American Association of New York, a satellite office for the Arab-American Family Support Center during the time of my research (now closed), Arab grocery stores and bakeries, and churches and mosques serving Arab religious communities. Map by Edmar Miglhorance.

Between Sixty-Eighth and Seventy-Third, the numbers ranged instead from a high of 52 percent to a low of 33 percent. This dropped to 6 percent of the next block, with nothing after Bay Ridge Parkway. Side streets off Fifth Avenue in this area often had several Arab stores; on Bay Ridge Avenue, a major cross street, 61 percent of the storefronts were marked as Arab. In addition, blocks with Arab stores tended to have very few other ethnicities marked on them. The two blocks before Sixty-Eighth had either a quarter or a third of their stores with signs indicating a particular immigrant nationality, but blocks with Arab stores had either zero or one store marked with a non-Arab nationality.

In December 2013, repeating my walk along Fifth, I noticed that the concentration of Arab-marked storefronts was expanding. Arab-marked businesses and community institutions began on Sixty-Seventh Street, including the shuttered offices of a Yemeni-American association, a social club for those from Beit Hanania, a Palestinian town in northern

Israel, and a Yemeni restaurant. New businesses had also arisen along the densely Arab core—a *shisha* (hookah) bar, with young Arab men, dressed for a night out, standing outside, and a new ice cream store with a pile of *Aramica* newspapers (a local Arabic-English free paper) outside. There were also scattered Arab-marked businesses past Seventy-Third Street—a pharmacy with Arabic-language signs between Seventy-Sixth and Seventy-Seventh, a halal Chinese restaurant on the same block, a restaurant on Seventy-Fourth Street right off Fifth Avenue. This gradual expansion has built from the existing core of the community and represents the flows that mark a dynamic urban community.

Beyond the storefronts along this strip, there are also a variety of institutions serving people of Arab descent throughout the neighborhood. After leaving first Manhattan and then Downtown Brooklyn, many Syrian/Lebanese Christians from the first wave of Arab immigrants settled in Bay Ridge. The most prominent legacy of their presence is their churches, such as St. Mary's Antiochian Orthodox Church and Fourth Avenue Presbyterian.[9] More recent additions to the Arab-centric religious landscape include Salam Lutheran Arabic Church, which shares space with an English-language Lutheran church on Eightieth Street, and the Islamic Society of Bay Ridge, which is located on the Fifth Avenue strip. As I mentioned above, the Arab American Association of New York, the institutional base for much of my fieldwork, has its offices on Fifth Avenue. The Arab-American Family Support Center, an older and less community-driven service organization for Arabs in New York, leased office space along Bay Ridge Avenue for a while during my fieldwork but has since returned to its office in Boerum Hill. Arab coffee shops and shisha bars provide public spaces for men, especially teens and students, to socialize and talk. All of these institutions provide the skeleton that supports the growth of a sense of shared community, where people see each other at jama'iyya (meaning the Arab American Association) programs, at the mosque or church, at the grocery store that stocks halal meat and Arab spices and ingredients, and in each other's houses to socialize, creating a densely interwoven set of relationships.

In addition, the areas right around Bay Ridge also have moderately high Arab populations: the zip codes for Sunset Park and Bensonhurst are 3.1 percent Arab, according to ACS data, and are also home to mosques, including the Muslim American Society in Bensonhurst, a major organizational locus for Muslim youth of all ethnicities. The Arabs living in these neighborhoods intermix with those living in Bay Ridge and are part of the same set of networks. Rather than growing their own networks and institutions, generally Arabs living in these neighborhoods use services available in Bay Ridge, with the notable exception of the Muslim American Society.

Outside of Bay Ridge, there are two other areas in New York that can be called Arab neighborhoods. Astoria, a diverse immigrant neighborhood in northern Queens, has a strong concentration of Egyptian, Moroccan, and other Arab immigrants and their families. The zip codes covering Astoria are about 3 percent Arab, with notable populations particularly of Egyptians and Moroccans visible in the ACS data and also substantial numbers of Lebanese and Arab respondents. However, very few foreign-born persons report being born in Lebanon or in Yemen (a major sending point for persons identifying as Arab), and a much higher number of the foreign-born report birth in Egypt or Morocco, which suggests that this is an immigrant community of Egyptians and Moroccans, with a smaller number of other US-born Arabs, perhaps beyond the second generation. The commercial core of the neighborhood is a several-block stretch of Steinway Street, with a number of Egyptian and other Arab restaurants and cafés, Arab groceries for sale in some shops, and at least one Arab-owned, but general in audience, supermarket. In addition, there are at least two mosques, a Coptic church, and an Arabic-speaking Protestant church in the neighborhood. Walking along Steinway between Astoria Boulevard and Twenty-Eighth Avenue, the prevailing scent in the air is of shisha smoke, and pastry shops and restaurants serving Arab food dominate the landscape. During the time of my fieldwork, the American MidEast Leadership Network, an organization whose primary mission was sending groups of citizen ambassadors to Syria and other Middle Eastern countries, opened an office to provide family services, including English classes and a youth program, but these programs were small in scale and by 2015 appeared to have ceased to exist. At the time of my research, interviewees described the community as very young, with few structured institutions and very little intracommunity trust. It is unclear if, in the intervening years, the community has developed further, but it has not further institutionalized itself the way Bay Ridge has.

The section of Boerum Hill around Atlantic Avenue in Downtown Brooklyn was a historic center of Arab community in New York during the first wave of Arab migration to the United States. Unlike Little Syria in Lower Manhattan, which was largely destroyed by subsequent waves of development, much of the infrastructure built by those immigrants remains, such as the Maronite cathedral. Arab-owned businesses, including bakeries, dry goods stores, and restaurants, intermix with other stores along a two-block stretch of Atlantic in proportions similar to those in Bay Ridge and Astoria. However, the Arab population in the area is very small, with only 1.3 percent of the Downtown Brooklyn population and 1.7 percent in Boerum Hill, the zip code to the east, giving an Arab ancestry. Downtown Brooklyn has a small Lebanese population, mostly US-born, and a slightly larger Yemeni-born population (who identify themselves mostly as Arab). Boerum Hill is home to a foreign-born Yemeni population, but both of these are very small, on the order of a few hundred individuals between both zip codes (which have a population of around a hundred thousand people). The actual number of people of Arab ancestry, or immigrants from Arab countries, may in fact be higher, but the community is numerically dwarfed by either Astoria or Bay Ridge. However, because of the historic association between Arabs and this neighborhood, the existence of stores and Arab churches, and the presence of the offices of the Arab-American Family Support Center, the first Arab American service organization in New York City, on Clinton Avenue, the Atlantic Avenue area remains strongly identified with Arab New Yorkers, despite the small size of its Arab population.

These three neighborhoods vary in terms of two important characteristics: whether there is a substantial population of people with Arab ancestry and whether there are institutions that are Arab identified. Downtown Brooklyn has institutional markers of Arab community but lacks a resident population of Arabs, although its central location means that those who want to use those institutions can get there easily. Astoria, by contrast, has a significant concentration of people of Arab descent, particularly North African immigrants, but is much more weakly institutionalized, with a commercial district the primary indicator of the community's presence. It is only Bay Ridge that has both a substantial Arab population and a strong and diverse set of Arab-identified institutions.

Beyond these hubs of Arab population and institutions, there are thousands of other people with Arab ancestry and immigrants from Arab countries throughout all five boroughs. They may be third-generation Syrian or Lebanese Christians, second-generation children of immigrants who are settled anywhere in the United States, or recent immigrants from any Arab country, but many of them still identify themselves as part of an Arab community, despite not living among a large number of fellow Arabs. For these individuals, Arab community may be found in artistic, cultural, or political action. Alternately, religious community may be more important than ethnic community. And, of course, there are many people of Arab descent or immigrant background whose Arab identity is tangential to their personal identity and who may not seek out a specific location of Arab community or may not seek it out regularly.

Arab Community Institutions

Civil society is the name given, at its most general, to those public activities that people engage in voluntarily but collectively. Iris Marion Young identifies three types of associations as making up civil society: private associations, for the benefit of their members; civic associations, for the benefit of a wider community; and political associations, which make specific demands on state or market institutions to change.[10] Young's definition of "political," relating to state or market institutions, strikes me as unnecessarily limiting for a definition of politics full stop, but does highlight a particular zone of the political—contestation against ruling institutions. While any kind of organization can be a fertile site for understanding everyday politics in a given moment, Young's framework still is useful as a way of understanding the purposes of a given organization and what ends it serves.

Private associations include, most significantly, religious institutions. Although religious institutions can serve a wide variety of civic functions, including charitable functions, providing space and opportunities for community groups, and supporting a broad sense of membership in the community as a whole, their key purpose is to serve their members, in terms of both religious purposes (providing a place for practicing necessary rites and rituals, some of which can be performed only as a group) as well as charitable and community functions that are specific to members or coreligionists. There are a wide variety of Arab churches in New York. Some, like the Melkite Church of the Virgin Mary in Park Slope, St. Mary's Antiochian Orthodox Church in Bay Ridge, the eight Coptic churches in Manhattan, Queens, Brooklyn, and Staten Island, and Our Lady of Lebanon Maronite Cathedral in Brooklyn Heights, represent indigenous Middle Eastern forms of Christian practice, while others, such as Fourth Avenue Presbyterian and Salam Lutheran Arabic Church (mentioned above), bring together Arab-heritage Protestant communities. In addition, there are dozens of mosques throughout the city. The most prominent mosques that serve Arab Muslims are the Islamic Society of Bay Ridge and the Muslim American Society Youth Center in Bensonhurst. Private associations also include social organizations, such as the Network of Arab-American Professionals (a networking organization for young professionals), the Salaam Club (a social club for Lebanese immigrants), or the Beit Hanania social club, mentioned above. Like religious institutions, they often cross the line between private and civic organizations by becoming involved in charitable activities directed at non–community members.

Political associations include organizations focused on both American and international politics. For example, there are a number of Palestine-focused groups with different ideologies and practices; below I discuss in detail the two most prominent, Al-Awda and Adalah-NY. (There are also pro-Palestinian groups that do not have Arab members or an Arab identity, such as Jews Against the Occupation, Jewish Voice for Peace, and the Women in Black Union Square vigil.) Other groups focus on other homeland issues, such as the Yemeni American Association of Bay Ridge and the Egyptian Alliance for Change, discussed in chapter 6.

At the time of my fieldwork, there was little organized attention being paid to electoral politics. Yalla Vote!, a voter-registration and get-out-the-vote project run by the AAI, a national organization, had a presence in the city during the 2008 election season, but there was no lasting presence for the group. Similarly, a local American-Arab Anti-Discrimination Committee (ADC) chapter had been in operation at one point in the city but was dormant during my fieldwork. In more recent years, domestic-focused political organizing has increased, with the Muslim Democratic Club of New York bringing together Muslims of multiple ethnic backgrounds, including prominent Arab Americans. While many individual Arabs in New York are interested and active in politics, collective, institutionalized, Arab-identified organizations that create specifically Arab spaces for that engagement in politics are few.

However, many of Arab New York's civic associations engage in activities that, in Young's terms, include strong political elements. The Arab American Association of New York is structured as a social services organization, teaching English to newcomers, helping with citizenship and benefits applications, and offering children's activities. But it also took on a central role in organizing against NYPD surveillance of Muslim and Arab communities in the city, encouraging voter registration and voting, and other clearly political activities. When I spoke with Linda Sarsour, its director, about these activities, she said that they did them out of necessity, not out of any particular interest in being political. "Honestly, if we'd had a functional ADC chapter we probably wouldn't have done any of it," she said, shrugging.[11] Similarly, Alwan for the Arts is nominally an arts organization, offering classes, talks, exhibits, and screenings of Arab, Middle Eastern, and Arab American visual and performing arts. However, it also frequently hosts political talks and panels and offers colloquial Arabic classes, which are frequented by pro-Palestine activists (Arab and not) wanting to improve their speaking skills. Even an organization like the Arab-American Family Support Center, which did not desire political engagement, ended up in political entanglements, such as in the complications related to its sponsorship of the Khalil Gibran International Academy, a specialized middle school that taught Arabic as a second language. Sometimes civic organizations (or even private institutions like religious groups) come to articulate the demands of their members and clients to power centers. Other times the issues they see as nonpolitical become politicized.

Research on civil society organizations—frequently framing them as "civic organizations," "nonprofits," or "community-based organizations"—has repeatedly emphasized their importance for people's political development. Social capital frameworks outline the ways that participation in these everyday spaces gives people the tools they need to become politically engaged: social networks, organizational skills, a sense of the common goods to be achieved through collective action.[12] Young argues specifically that civil society activity is necessary for self-determination, the ability to direct one's own life and make one's own choices.[13] And research has shown that for immigrants in particular community organizations are essential to their political socialization and incorporation.[14]

Because of the centrality of community-based organizations to immigrant political life as well as their function as defined, named organizations that can serve as bridges into the community for an outsider researcher, I chose to begin my fieldwork with them. My primary field site was the Arab American Association of New York, one of the most prominent Arab community organizations in New York City. The Arab American Association was founded in 2001 and has been providing services to the Arab community of Bay Ridge from its office on Fifth Avenue since then. On its website it describes its mission as "to support and empower the Arab Immigrant and Arab American community by providing services to help them adjust to their new home and become active members of society. Our aim is for families to achieve the ultimate goals of independence, productivity and stability."[15] The AAA is a 501(c)(3) nonprofit and funds its work through a mixture of grants from progressive foundations, grants from the New York City and New York State governments, program-specific partnerships with health care companies, and private donations, particularly from within the Arab community.

In 2009, when I began volunteering at the AAA, it was well established as a community service center. The majority of its staff were hired under the aegis of AmeriCorps and AmeriCorps VISTA, two federal government programs that fund living stipends for volunteers working in community service. AAA's caseworkers assisted clients with welfare benefits, immigration paperwork, relations with the police, and other means of interfacing with the bureaucratic state; much of their work consisted of translation and filling in forms. It also offered English classes targeted specifically at women, which brought in large (if variable) numbers of recent immigrants, as well as citizenship exam preparation. There were also a variety of youth programs, including after-school homework help, teen programs, specific programming for both young and teenaged girls, and teen volunteering and service programs. In addition, they have formed strategic relationships with hospitals and insurance companies to target health-related programming at Arabs, including frequent health workshops.

At the time of my fieldwork, the majority of the staff of the AAA came from the Bay Ridge community and had few or no credentials to support their work apart from prior volunteering experience. They included high school, college, and graduate students. Most grew up in Arabic-speaking households, were Muslim, and lived in Bay Ridge. The VISTA employees had more formal experience and were specifically there to better institutionalize the organization. But the value that came with being a long-term volunteer and participant in Arab community life was rewarded highly in this phase of the organization's development.

Since my time doing fieldwork with the AAA there have been two major changes. The first is the increased professionalization of the staff. After the wave of staff from Bay Ridge whom I worked for, the next wave largely consisted of non–New Yorkers, mostly recent college graduates with a scholarly or personal commitment to Arab communities or the Middle East, but not with roots in Bay Ridge or other New York Arab communities. Since then, the staff has turned over several times, particularly because the AmeriCorps program has stopped funding the staff members (who were, by their nature, temporary). More members of the current staff have roots in Arab communities in New York than in the period immediately after my fieldwork, although there are still more non-Arab individuals and non–New Yorkers on staff now than there were when I worked there. But all of the employees are considerably more professionally qualified: only one is a college student, several have preimmigration degrees and certificates from their countries of origin along with US tertiary credentials, and several are recent college graduates from selective American schools (City College, University of Michigan, NYU, Swarthmore College).

The second change in the AAA's practices since I started working there is their increasingly critical engagement in politics. At my first interview with Sarsour, in 2009, she spoke of good relationships with city council members and get-out-the-vote work in the 2008 elections and of conversations about the 2008 Israeli bombardment of Gaza in ESL classes. A city council member came to open and close the summer youth program I volunteered with, took the kids on a tour of City Hall, and presented all the program's volunteers with certificates of appreciation. On the walls of the AAA office are several maps of Palestine, labeled in Arabic, produced by activist organizations. Once when I was hanging out at the office, a staff member came around with a large bag of narrow *kuffiyehs* (the kind worn for protests, not the authentic version) that he had found in the basement; he did not explain to me where they came from, but did complain that he wished he had found them before the previous weekend's protest. Perhaps they had been bought to distribute at pro-Palestine rallies, or perhaps they had been stored there by a volunteer or staff member who was active in pro-Palestine activism. In any case, the idea that a bag of kuffiyehs—a frequently controversial object for Palestinians and their supporters in the United States—was a proper thing to have in the AAA was perfectly acceptable to everyone who saw it. Throughout my fieldwork, the organization's approach to politics was embodied in the idea that engagement with the city government and institutions could be productive, a standard civic duty narrative about voting and participation, and an interest in and engagement with Middle Eastern politics among staff and service users.

After my fieldwork ended, it was revealed that the NYPD had been involved in aggressive profiling and surveilling of the Arab and Muslim communities in New York under the guise of "antiterrorism." As part of the incredibly hostile reaction to this revelation among Arabs in the city, the AAA (one of the NYPD's targets) began to engage more heavily with advocates for civil liberties, antiracist groups, and other progressive political movements. When I reinterviewed Sarsour in 2014, she spoke about the absolute necessity for the AAA to get involved in politics—in part because there weren't other organizations within the Arab community in New York that were willing to take on these issues. Indeed, she has risen to national prominence as a left-wing Muslim organizer, including as a spokesperson in anti–police brutality organizations, in part through her work with the AAA. Middle Eastern politics still matters greatly to people at the AAA, but their focus has been redirected to a newly conflictual relationship with local and national state power.

The Arab American Association was crucial to my understanding of the politics of Arab immigrant communities. I was brought into the organization very rapidly, once I had expressed an interest in research and volunteering. Linda was the first person to agree to be interviewed by me as I began research. When I asked her if I could come see the office and mentioned that I might like to volunteer, she told me to stop by anytime. When I did, I was introduced to the development director, a young non-Arab man. During our first conversation, he talked me through the entire staff, explained their job descriptions, handed me any copies of public documents on the AAA he could find, and introduced me to the assistant director, the adult education coordinator, and the youth programs coordinator. The development director suggested to the adult education coordinator that I would like to volunteer with the women's ESL class, which seemed to be the way many volunteers began their careers at the AAA. By the next week I was teaching a group of basic English learners once a week. During my time at the AAA, I taught ESL once or twice a week, in a variety of different classroom formats, frequently without supervision or direction. Staff were friendly and chatty, both with me and with each other in my presence, were willing to hand me extra copies of organizational documents (like volunteer rosters and time cards), and let me hang out in their offices to listen to them fight, complain, and, occasionally, work. Over the course of my fieldwork, I continued to teach ESL, initially to beginning students, eventually to advanced students. I also volunteered at special events, such as the annual Earth Day cleanup, several of the youth programs, and the annual bazaar that was a part of Arab American heritage week.

Although much of my fieldwork was conducted during these programs and in my observations of the functioning of the organization, for me the AAA was most often an entrée to the community of Bay Ridge. It provided me with regular contact and time to build relationships with members of the immigrant community, including those who were recent arrivals, had limited English ability, or were children and youth. Those personal connections to participants in the AAA's programming were an essential component of my research because they allowed me to have interlocutors who had a broader view of the life of the community than I did.

At the beginning of my research I also approached an older and more professionalized Arab community organization, the Arab-American Family Support Center (AAFSC), located on Clinton Street near Atlantic Avenue. The AAFSC was founded by a former city social worker who felt there was a strong need for linguistically and culturally competent social services within the Administration for Children's Services (ACS) system. The organization received the majority of its funding from the New York City government, acting as a subcontractor for providing services to families in the child welfare system. In addition, they provided English classes, youth activities, and assistance with obtaining medical insurance and applying for welfare benefits. Unlike the AAA, they employed a large staff of highly professionally qualified social workers and other community workers, including those who spoke languages other than Arabic, to serve non-Arab, non-Anglophone clients referred to them through ACS (a requirement of their contract with them).

In addition, the AAFSC was the major community partner for the Khalil Gibran International Academy, a public middle school that aimed to teach Arabic and English and bring together Arabic-speaking students with other students whose parents wanted them to develop Arabic skills. (New York has a variety of these schools for Chinese, Spanish, and other languages.) Openly racist and Islamophobic opposition to the school ended up poisoning the project, as did highly personal attacks on the chosen principal, Debbie Almontaser (as detailed in the first chapter). During the time of my research, the school was operational and the initial furor had died down, but the school was already on the rocky path that would lead to its closing a few years later.

I met with a total of four staff members from the AAFSC in an attempt to gain permission to carry out more detailed research on their work and to be able to learn about their clients and participants in their programs. However, I was unsuccessful. Much of the reason for this, I believed at the time, had to do with the organization's powerfully negative experience of politics in the wake of the KGIA fiasco and an unwillingness to be engaged with through that framework. When I told staff members that I was studying "political discourse" in Arab communities, I was immediately told, "We are a social services organization, we don't deal with politics." (In fact, during one conversation, the interviewee misread the name of my graduate institution—the New School for Social Research—as the New School for Social Services, in what struck me as a fairly Freudian slip.) I was told that "Arabs don't care about politics," a statement that struck me then and continues to strike me as absurd on its face, but which I read as saying that the organization and the communities it serves are more interested in success and survival in the American context than in any sort of conflict with power centers. When I mentioned the possibility of volunteering, I was gently brushed aside. I was never directly shut down, but the contrast to the AAA was very apparent.

I chose not to continue with my research into the AAFSC, as much as I was interested in their different experience. Fundamentally, such research felt nonconsensual; although the organization did have a public face and was willing to put out some information, I felt as if it would be inappropriate to keep poking an organization so clearly uninterested in the questions that interested me and so deeply wary after its involuntary exposure during the KGIA fiasco.

It is likely that my data would have been different if I had been able to learn more about the internal dynamics of the AAFSC. For instance, it is very possible that their clients differ meaningfully from those at the AAA. First, government referrals send many clients to the AAFSC, meaning that they do not choose the organization as a way of being a part of an Arab community in practice, though inertia and familiarity might keep them there and involve them in other, voluntary programs. Second, clients may choose the AAFSC over the AAA because of the organization's more professionalized and less political orientation. The AAA is deeply imbedded in neighborhood and community networks, where people know and remember each other. Someone who needed services in Arabic but wanted to avoid either a particular individual or a general tendency might go to the AAFSC instead. (Alternately, people might choose the AAA because they like or trust individuals or networks that run through there or because of their more politicized attitude and different power bases.) It is entirely possible that the processes that build an Arab community in practice take different forms in these two different environments. Testing the frameworks and processes used to understand the data I was able to gather in the AAA is a comparative exercise that I leave for other researchers to explore more fully than I was able to.

While immigrant-serving community-based organizations are a key site where an Arab American community can be produced, I wanted to explore other such sites. Another key area of political socialization and action that matters to both everyday politics and the lived experience of Arab American politics is social movement activity. As the Detroit Arab American Survey showed, Arab Detroiters are more likely than non-Arab Detroiters to have attended a protest, the only form of political engagement where Arabs participated more than their neighbors.[16] Naber's research on what she calls the Leftist Arab Movement in the San

Francisco Bay Area also demonstrates the ways in which Arab communities center on social movement activity, making it a priority of their experience.[17] This is unusual for immigrants as well as for other Americans, for whom social movement participation usually lags behind other political participation.[18]

The two social movement organizations I chose to focus on were Adalah-NY: The New York Campaign for the Boycott of Israel and Al-Awda NY: The Palestine Right to Return Coalition. That both of them focused on pro-Palestinian advocacy was not random: as mentioned above, at the time of my research, the only consistent social movement activity within the Arab American community was centered on Palestinian rights. I chose to focus on them for two reasons. First, they were the two most prominent pro-Palestine organizations with an Arab identity within the city. Although there are non-Arab members in both organizations, both have a substantial number of members who are themselves Arab identified and integrate Arab political identities into their work. Second, the two organizations draw from very different parts of the Arab communities of the city. While Adalah-NY draws from both immigrant and second-generation professionals who work as part of New York's knowledge economy, Al-Awda draws from the recently immigrated residents of ethnic enclaves.[19] These two patterns of bringing together Arab-identified people for activism for Palestine struck me as a useful set of contrasts that could be theoretically fruitful.

Adalah-NY was founded in 2006, in the aftermath of the Israeli attack on Lebanon, and was originally named Adalah-New York: Coalition for Justice in the Middle East. Members who formed it were generally experienced in anti-Zionist and pro-Palestinian advocacy. In November 2007, Adalah-NY began to shift its focus away from generalized Palestine advocacy and toward the Boycott, Divestment, and Sanctions (BDS) movement, in response to a call from many major Palestinian civil society organizations to focus on BDS. In the period after the Gaza bombardment in January 2009, several members of Adalah-NY worked with other activists to form the New York Campaign for the Boycott of Israel, with the intention of becoming a coalition organization of pro-BDS groups. However, in February 2010, the two groups merged, or rather reintegrated, as at least half of NYCBI's members were already members of Adalah-NY. The new merged group took on the name of Adalah-NY: The New York Campaign for the Boycott of Israel.

Adalah-NY's hallmark is the small-scale creative protest, usually with around forty people in attendance and songs, skits, and chants relevant to the protest theme. Their major campaign during my fieldwork advocated boycott and divestment from Lev Leviev, an Israeli jeweler and real estate mogul who funds the building of settlements and whose company, Africa-Israel, can also be tied to human rights violations in Africa. NYC-BI's major campaign had been advocating for a boycott of Motorola, which manufactures military equipment for the Israel Defense Forces. However, this campaign had tapered out by February 2009 and was formally eliminated after the merger. In addition, Adalah-NY organized protests advocating for the cultural boycott of Israeli artistic institutions, such as the Israel Ballet and the Batsheva Dance Company, which was a growing part of their work and seemed to be their next major focus. Adalah-NY was also routinely invited to join coalitions with other activist groups and held other protests in connection with these groups, and Adalah-NY members also attended other major Palestine protests.

Adalah-NY has perhaps thirty core members who attend meetings regularly and organize actions. The core members are nearly all college graduates with professional jobs, although there are several college students, from Columbia and NYU, who do attend. Most live in Manhattan or Brooklyn, but not in Arab immigrant neighborhoods. The group contains a large number of members who are Arab, both US-born and immigrant. However, both immigrant and US-born Arabs are similar in that they do not have family ties in New York. Immigrants came to the United States as adults, for education or for work, and their families remain in their countries of origin (mainly Palestine and Lebanon). American-born Arabs have family elsewhere in the United States and moved to the city for school or work, like many highly educated, middle- and upper-class New Yorkers of all backgrounds. Adalah-NY also has a significant number of members who are Jewish, all of European/Ashkenazi origin. There are also non-Jewish, non-Arab members. Arab and non-Arab members are similar to each other in class and professional background and share experience both in pro-Palestine/anti-Zionist organizing and in other social movements and the nonprofit sector.

Members' experience in other organizations is a large part of what constructs Adalah-NY's activist network. Adalah-NY members organize Israeli Apartheid Week and are active in or have had ties to a variety of Jewish anti-occupation groups as well as other antiwar and social justice organizations. Adalah-NY is often recruited into working on particular campaigns by other organizations, such as Arab American groups like NAAP-NY and ADC (nationally, not the NYC branch) or an expansive list of progressive and left-wing organizations. The groups they affiliate with are often more progressive than radical, even though Adalah-NY would identify itself as a radical political group. A significant number of members are Jewish identified, and very few of them have a "people of color" identity.

Relatively early in my research I interviewed two Arab American members of Adalah-NY about the organization and their work, which cemented my interest in them, as members spoke openly both about their political thinking and about differences in identities and political orientations among Arabs in New York. Therefore, I approached them about joining the group to conduct participant-observation fieldwork. They agreed, and I began attending meetings in October 2009, first at an "open meeting" for new members (described more in chapter 5). I continued attending planning meetings and demonstrations until April 2010, along with participating in their internal organizing listserv. Since I stopped active participation, I have continued to follow the group electronically and communicate occasionally with members, both personally and with regard to their work.

Al-Awda NY: The Palestine Right to Return Coalition is connected to the national Al-Awda network, which has chapters in many major cities, particularly in California and Chicago. However, New York's branch is autonomous, and, according to leaders, more of its members and leaders come from working-class backgrounds, and they frame their struggle as being based in class politics and working-class perspectives. Al-Awda, whose name means "return," is organized around the right of Palestinians to return to their homes or ancestral homes, both in the West Bank and Gaza and within the territory that is now Israel. They also tend to organize protests and events around the critical issues of the moment. For instance, Al-Awda was one of the leading organizations in the Break the Siege on Gaza Coalition, a group that organized the largest of New York's demonstrations against the Israeli invasion of Gaza in December 2008, with several thousand people in attendance. In fact, in July 2009, the Facebook fan page for the Break the Siege on Gaza Coalition became the Al-Awda NY Facebook fan page. In addition to large-scale protests, Al-Awda also hosts fund-raisers for aid to Palestinian refugees and others and educational events, sometimes at universities, sometimes at leftist activist spaces.

Attendance at Al-Awda events largely comes from the borough communities of Bensonhurst and Bay Ridge, along with the Arab communities of Paterson, New Jersey, and elsewhere in the periphery of New York. Often people attend in family groups, and many speak Arabic among themselves during demonstrations. The organization is led by a small group of organizers. The most regularly acknowledged leader, who frequently acts as event MC, is a young woman in her late twenties or early thirties, a lawyer with an office on Fifth Avenue in Bay Ridge and another in Manhattan. Leaders who speak from the podium at events or march at the head of the demonstration include adult men from Bay Ridge and Bensonhurst's Arab community who hold respected jobs in the community, such as doctors and lawyers, and a large contingent of college and high school students, referred to as "the generation of Gaza," teenage children of immigrant Arabs who became involved in activism after the 2008 bombardment of Gaza.

Al-Awda has a large network of organizations that cosponsor demonstrations and events with them and who sometimes send leaders to speak at events. During my fieldwork, they included black nationalist and other ethnic radical organizations, radical labor movements, several Muslim organizations, the International Jewish Anti-Zionist Movement, and the International Action Center, which is best known for being the sponsoring organization for ANSWER, one of the two major post 9/11 antiwar movements in the United States. Organizations that allied with Al-Awda tended to identify themselves as radical, and many of them had a "people of color" identity. It also has many more connections in Muslim- and Arab-identified community organizations, such as the Palestine Community Network and the American Muslim Federation for Palestine.

I first learned of Al-Awda as a college student, around the time of its formation; other students on my Connecticut campus knew of it and its leaders and connected antiwar and pro-Palestine campus organizers to it. When I moved to New York, I took a community Arabic class at

Alwan, whose other students were Palestinian Americans working on improving their language skills to support their political work in Palestine. They invited me to join Al-Awda, which they were involved in, but I declined as I was trying to focus on my upcoming graduate school career rather than organizing. So when I began researching Palestine activism in New York, Al-Awda was a familiar organization, and I sought it out in order to see how it related to the broader Arab community. I attended Al-Awda protests and public events from January 2009 until January 2010. However, I had great difficulty connecting with leaders in the movement. Unlike Adalah-NY, which was responsive to outsiders, Al-Awda did not prioritize contact with nonparticipants. Despite repeated online and face-to-face contact, I was unable to schedule an interview with a member until November 2013, long after my core fieldwork was over. However, the content of that conversation syncs with the data I collected through observation and participation in demonstrations and public events as well as analysis of documents produced by the group and publicly available.[20]

Conclusion

My picture of Arab New York is not complete: no picture could be. My limits were set in part by who I am—a non-Arab, a non-Muslim, a woman, an itinerant participant in the specific social spaces where I located my research. They were also set by the spaces in which I worked: secular groups (or at least groups not focused on religious practice) engaged in public civil society activities, based in different subsections of the Arab community. But they provide a lens through which to think about the ways that politics works in the everyday spaces of Arab New York. In addition, in all three of the key organizations in which I worked, participants struggled, sometimes together and sometimes at odds with each other, with the limits and compulsions of being able to engage with politics and the broader public sphere as Arab Americans, from their own standpoints and experiences. In the next chapter, I explore how spaces that are read by outsiders as nonpolitical can provide a particular opportunity to develop and affirm Arab identities and a notion of Arab community in ways that minimize the problems caused by explicit political engagement.

PART II

Everyday Contestations

3

Making 'Arabiya

Education and Identity

My coteacher Dan and I were sitting around a table on the second floor of the Arab American Association offices on Fifth Avenue in Bay Ridge, Brooklyn, with six of our students from the intermediate English as a second language class. All of the women were recent immigrants from the Arab world, mothers with young children, and Muslims who wore headscarves. This being a room full of New Yorkers, we were complaining about how high rent is.

Hanan abruptly changed the topic. "It's very expensive to live *fi blad* [in the homeland]," she said. "It costs too much with the salaries. A government worker, he might make three hundred dollars a month, but you have four or five kids, you spend three hundred dollars a week." The women around the table began to nod in agreement. She continued, "It's because the government takes your money and just puts it in their pocket, doesn't give it back to the people," again to the approval of her audience. The women went on to discuss their experiences with corruption: bribes for papers of all sorts, embezzlement, bureaucratic red tape. Dan slowly filled the whiteboard with vocabulary words: corruption, nepotism, bribe, pragmatic, ideal.

When we think about educational spaces, we tend to assume that they are nonpolitical. What happens in the classroom is about teaching people skills and preparing them for careers and life in common. When we talk about politicizing education, we frequently mean imposing external political demands that alter the "pure" educational value of curriculum, such as Christian opposition to the teaching of evolution or the emphasis on diversity in place of the Western canon. If we think at all about serving political goals through the classroom, we assume that educational spaces are intended to prepare people to participate in political life. Hannah Arendt describes this binary nicely in her essay "What Is

Authority?": "In the political realm we deal always with adults who are past the age of education, properly speaking, and politics or the right to participate in the management of public affairs begins precisely where education has come to an end. . . . In education, conversely, we always deal with people who cannot yet be admitted to politics and equality because they are being prepared for it."[1]

But educational spaces are, in fact, fertile ground for everyday political engagement. The stated purpose of an educational space is the exploration of knowledge, the testing of propositions, and the interrogation of ideas—processes that are central to people's political lives. Within those spaces, people have room to talk and think about the world around them. In this chapter, I show how community educational spaces are crucial for the development of a collective Arab identity among recent immigrants and their children. The staff who organize community educational spaces and the adults and children who participate in them collectively make space for ongoing engagements with what it means to be an Arab immigrant to the United States. Specifically, participants in those spaces emerge from them with a well-developed notion of common Arab identity, which I call 'arabiya (Arabness), as opposed to local, religious, or national origin identities. They also gain practice articulating that identity in a dialectical relationship to Americanness, both opposed to and coexisting with it.

Collectively held political identities are a central prerequisite for political engagement. If we lack a political identity, one that enables us to locate ourselves in the political body of our community and helps others understand and interpret us, we end up struggling to speak to our fellow citizens and convince them to listen to us. Our identities are not naturally given to us—we come to inhabit them through political processes of contestation, through ongoing processes of identity formation. As Courtney Jung argues, "Before there could be a Latino political voice, or a 'Latino vote' to court, the category of 'Latinos' had to be constructed as a group with common interests, a common sensibility, and a history of immigration, conquest, marginalization, etc. It is only with the establishment of this political identity as Latinos that individuals could be bounded by ethnicity to develop political agency and, as a corollary, the critical capacity to contest a particular form of ethnic, linguistic and maybe even racial discrimination."[2] Similarly, the category of "Arab

American" needs to be constructed from the experiences of people of Arab descent in order to make it possible for actors understood as Arab American, whether individual or collective, to take action.

The role of educational spaces for identity development and formation is particularly important for Arab Americans because of how limited the space is for them to explore and develop a collective identity. The forms of racism, Islamophobia, anti-immigrant bias, and assimilationist pressure present in American society make it hard for Arabs to be Arab in mixed company and mean that when they choose to do so, they must engage in forms of interrogation and often profound misrecognition that limit how they can express and debate what it means to be Arab. But community educational spaces that are mostly directed and populated by people who self-identify as Arab in one way or another allow some of that to be avoided and the practical discourses people share with each other to proceed with fewer constraints and more freedom. The ever-present threat of discursive misrecognition, in particular, is reduced in a context where most participants share a similar background, which makes the active work of participating in dialogue with others more straightforward and less perilous.

During my time at the AAA, I participated in two educational programs, both of which were major programming efforts for the organization. The first was the women-only English as a second language classes, which met four days a week. The structure of the classes ebbed and flowed as volunteers and students came and went, but I participated in three different moments in the classes' history. First, I taught introductory English, while Dan, a non-Arab who had been volunteering for a while, taught intermediate English; second, I partnered with Dan (and prepared to take over his class when he left to join the Peace Corps) in the intermediate class, while Sara, a bilingual recent immigrant from Jordan, taught introductory English; third, Dan's students departed after he left, and I either cooperated with Sara in her introductory class or assisted Samira, a former intermediate student, in teaching a bilingual basic English/Arabic literacy class to a small number of older women. The content and structure of the classes were entirely unconstrained by AAA staff, which meant teachers and students were free to explore as they wished.

The summer program provided low-cost child care to elementary-school-aged children and was held three days a week (in the same space as the ESL class—in fact, the ESL class changed its schedule to accommodate the children). Children attended from morning until afternoon, and their days included fieldtrips, crafts, and scheduled culture days. The program was organized by two AAA staff members, and the majority of the labor for it came from young adults who participated in the Summer Youth Employment Project, a city grant-based program. I was the only adult volunteer, though my friend and age-peer Suleikha was the director. I was also the only white person involved with the program, though not the only non-Arab.

These programs were a rich environment in which participants, who chose to prioritize and invest in an Arab identity through their participation in these activities at this center, came to develop the framework for collective identity I call ʿarabiya. I use the term ʿarabiya, literally "Arabness," for two reasons. One, I am borrowing from the fact that many of the women and children I worked with in these programs would use the word ʿarabi, rather than the English word "Arab," to identify members of an Arab community. (For instance, a woman in the ESL class trying to figure out why an obviously non-Arab person was working at the center asked if my husband was ʿarabi. I said no and didn't bother to clarify that I have a wife and not a husband.) In this spirit, I use the term to identify the discourse they are developing. Second, I use it in a gesture toward the politics of pan-Arabism, a popular political ideology in the twentieth-century Middle East, which advocated for the cultural and political unity of the entire Arab region.[3] Pan-Arabism, with its principle of singular Arab identity and goal of a united Arab people across all boundaries, was never successfully able to overcome the massive challenges it faced in practically uniting the huge numbers of people and distances of territory that could have led to the creation of a united Arab state, but it did help encourage people across the Arab world to identify with other Arabs from other places as part of a cultural whole. In diaspora, the familiarity of this discourse works to support practices that help create a collective, panethnic Arab identity out of what might have been individual Arab nationality-based identities.

In the rest of this chapter, I explore how the practice of ʿarabiya is developed and how participants in the educational spaces at the Arab American Association use it. Beginning with the ESL students, I explore how intra-Arab differences are negotiated to allow students to identify as members of an Arab collectivity, and how they turn their preliminary collective identification as ʿarabi (Arab) into a nuanced, practical community identity. Second, I turn to the way that ʿarabiya is positioned in dialogue with Americanness, both in the bodies of American teachers and in the understood common environment of New York and the United States. After examining how adults make and shape ʿarabiya, I look at the summer program, to see how the children of the women developing these notions of ʿarabiya enact them again in a space defined as Arab. I found that while prescriptive ʿarabiya that aims to shape young Arab Americans as properly disciplined Arab subjects collapses in the actual practice of the program, the children in the program actively engage in movement between forms of ʿarabiya and Americanness, inhabiting a discursive space that is comfortable being both Arab and American.

Making ʿArabiya

The English classes I taught were specifically for Arab immigrant women learning and practicing English, and there were never more than thirty students involved with the program at a time. However, despite this narrow population, there was tremendous diversity among the students. They ranged in age from their seventies to their twenties. All but a very small number were married with children, but their children varied in age from toddlers to fully grown adults. Some had worked outside the home before immigrating, while others never had; some had had university educations in the Arab world, while some were illiterate in Arabic as well as English. Nearly all were Muslim and wore the hijab, but they wore it differently, some with Western clothes and some with Arabic jilbabs or abayas. And, very importantly, they came from a wide variety of countries and places of origin, including both cities and small towns in Jordan, Lebanon, Egypt, Palestine, and Yemen.

The introductory class led by Sara and me, for instance, was largely composed of older women whose formal education in English was very limited, most of them coming from either Palestine or Yemen. One morning during introductory class, Sara and I were interrupted by a surprise from our Yemeni students: they had prepared breakfast for the entire class and the staff of the AAA. The table was cleared of worksheets and covered with food: one student brought a large loaf of croissant-like bread, baked in a pan that resembled a deep-dish pizza pan, with honey on top, while a mother/daughter pair brought salad, meat on the bone cooked with basmati rice, and their crowning achievement, ʿaseed, a polenta-like porridge that is served with broth and multiple sauces. The Yemeni women, including several who did not bring food, began serving the Palestinians, as well as Sara and me. (This seemed like a bad time to mention I'm a vegetarian, so I didn't.) I had never had ʿaseed before, so a large plate was made up for me, topped precisely with broth from a thermos, fenugreek foam, and a salsa-like tomato sauce, and I was given instructions for how to eat my dishes: "This [the ʿaseed], eat hot. That [my plate of salad and bread], okay cold." Discussion was excited, cheerful, and entirely in Arabic. Office staff, none of whom were Yemeni, came up to gather plates and were excited about getting to have ʿaseed. After we had all eaten and cleaned up, the daughter of the mother/daughter pair (herself married with young children) casually explained, in Arabic, how one makes ʿaseed. The conversation ended with the Palestinians and Yemenis discussing favorite dishes from each other's cuisines and cooking for weddings and holidays.

This was a profoundly cross-cultural moment for the Arab students and staff. ʿAseed is a dish that has no parallel in Levantine cuisine, and the bread, meat, and rice all differed subtly from their Levantine cousins. (Salad is roughly the same everywhere in the Arabic-speaking world.) However, the way the students engaged with each other across the meal was not about demarcating difference. Instead, the meal functioned as a way of bridging those differences. What was articulated through that pot of ʿaseed and the conversations around its sharing was the form of identity I describe as ʿarabiya.

This notion of ʿarabiya did not arise naturally. Instead, it was constructed actively (though perhaps not always consciously) by the women in the class. Throughout the classes I taught, students used a variety of discourses to invoke and develop this notion of ʿarabiya. One way of doing this was through the way students talked about their countries of origin. While the students' nationalities varied, and even students from the same country came from different cities and villages, students articulated their memories of their places of origin in ways that marked them as similar, not different. The linguistic device they used to do this was the notion of the *bilad/blad,* or homeland. When talking in English with teachers, students rarely identified their countries of origin by name and specified only when necessary. Instead, they spoke of "in my country," "*fi biladi*," or "*fi blad*" (in my country, in [the] homeland.) The blad here served to provide them with a common origin, which they all shared.

Even something as simple as a conversation about the weather could serve to structure this notion of a common blad. On a cool and rainy April day in a long string of them, the intermediate class drifted into a conversation about the weather and climate back home. Students began painting a picture of their idyllic country, where the sun warmed them—not like the sun in the United States, which is weak and does nothing. They described the fog rising in the morning over villages, family houses with courtyards of fruit trees, making drinks from flowers and herbs that grew in their gardens. Collectively, they painted a picture of a shared home, the same set of courtyards, gardens, and sunny days. Although a few women talked about national landmarks, such as the ruins at Petra or the pyramids, the conversation drew on a common image of the beautiful blad, which stood in stark contrast to the gray, wet, chilly picture outside our window.

The students also used social practices that they shared to evoke a common blad. Foodways could be a way of doing this. During the Yemeni breakfast in the introductory class, the conversation emphasized what women prepared for special occasions and the importance of national dishes, which allowed them to share a notion of collectivity. In the intermediate class, there were repeated conversations about where to find the right ingredients to cook Arab foods, and one class was turned over to the collective writing of a recipe for how to cook fish "the Arab way," with the women first arguing in Arabic about *the* way to prepare the fish and then painstakingly back-translating the agreed-upon recipe into English.

Because nearly all of the women in the class were Muslim, they would also use discourses around Islam to help bridge across local identities and make a version of 'arabiya strong enough to include everyone in the group. Samira's Arabic class concluded every week with the writing and recitation of a line from the Qur'an. The lines were never controversial points of theology but basic concepts like praising God, submission to his will, and forgiveness and charity toward others. After a session of learning to read basic vocabulary words, the women in the class would painstakingly copy the poetic language of the Qurʾan, recite the lines along with Samira, and listen to her brief sermons on the topic of the quote, which she would then translate into English for my benefit. Similarly, differences in social practice between the United States and the Middle East were ascribed to Islam, such as when students told us (giggling a little, as if it was scandalous but also titillating) that getting pregnant before marriage "isn't against your [Americans'] religion."

Given that Muslim identity is explicitly transnational and that there is a conscious rhetoric within many varieties of contemporary Islam about all believers being equal, Islam is a territory that some Arabs in the United States can rely upon for the building of an identity that transcends national origin. However, while Islam was never explicitly used in my hearing to exclude non-Muslims, it did create an effect of downplaying the role of Arab Christians in Arab communities—which may be a reason why very few Arab Christian immigrants participated in events at the AAA or in other, non-Christian-marked community groups.

ʿArabi, Not American: Dialogical Relationships

ʿArabiya was a part of the ongoing discourse within the ESL classroom. But while it worked in part by finding commonalities and emphasizing them among students' different experiences, it also worked by defining itself against Americanness. Particularly from the students' perspective, America was both the terrain and the topic of the course. Class materials, both natural texts like comic strips and professionally produced ESL materials, were clearly situated within the American cultural milieu, including material like children celebrating Valentine's Day (which, according to the women in classes, is only for married couples in the Middle East), sketches of people dressed in bathing suits discussing how hot it was (which led Samira to comment, laughing, that "you get hotter if you're naked like that"), or even simply the names of American cities, which students often were not familiar with. The students absorbed the need to put the language they used into their American context. Samira taught her basic English class the sentence "I buy pita," and then paused to explain in Arabic that pita was what you called *khubz* (Arab bread) in English, that it was the Greek name.

The women in the class were not anti-American in any meaningful sense of the word. They were pleased to live in the United States and even generally spoke positively about its government. As they discussed their lives here, it was clear that what they approved of was the functional state apparatus of living in America: a noncorrupt government, a functioning economy, free and adequate public education. As in Hanan's digression into talking about corruption back home at the beginning of this chapter, or a long discussion between Samira and Randa about the effects of structural adjustment on the economies in their countries, students compared the United States to their countries of origin and found that they preferred to be governed in the former.

This approval might seem counterintuitive, particularly given both government surveillance of Arab Americans and the effects of US foreign policy in the Middle East. But students were not responding to these meta-conditions; they were not engaged in the formal political system, and most had arrived too recently to have been subjected to the immediate post-9/11 actions against Arab Americans. The depth of NYPD surveillance of Muslim communities was still unrevealed, and relations between Arab communities in New York and city institutions were fairly good on the surface. The American state that these women judged was what they experienced in their everyday encounters with governmentality. They came to know the state when they took their children to public school, received benefits for low-income families such as food stamps or medical insurance, or sent their sons to be a part of the NYPD-sponsored soccer league. The American state these women saw was one that provided basic services to residents and benefits to the poor and needy, gave their children a reasonably good education for free, picked up their garbage, and maintained their parks. They contrasted this to their states of origin, which have failing social welfare systems, poor public education and financially burdensome private schools, and shoddy infrastructure, and emerged with the impression that America is better.

But this positive evaluation of the US state did not mean that students were interested in assimilating entirely into American society. In fact, the students specifically denied any interest in assimilation during a conversation that Dan led in the intermediate class. Randa spoke first and said that she thought assimilation was a very bad thing: "You lose your culture." Dan talked about people he knew, including his Vietnamese grandmother, who refused to talk to their kids in their mother tongues. The students were horrified by this prospect. "You have to give them your culture," Randa said. Then Dan asked, "What if someone moved to Jordan or Egypt from India? What should they do?" The class consensus was clear: you have to learn the language of the place you're living so you can communicate, but you have to keep your own culture, keep your own language, teach it to your kids.

This meant that students were able to use Americanness as an Other to ʿarabiya. Just as they could use the idea of the blad or pan-Islamic rhetoric to bring themselves together into a collectivity, they could also use their difference from Americans, including those Americans in the room, to construct that collectivity. Katherine Cramer argues that out-groups become increasingly salient in political talk when they are either physically present or introduced in representation, via the media or other artifacts that are present.[4] Dan and I were the physically present members of the out-groups, which allowed us to be the site of a transformation of Americanness from a monolithic cultural entity into a dialogue partner, something that could be interrogated and asked to give reasons, as we frequently were. The students were conscious of our out-group status: once during a discussion of child-raising practices, one woman explained her dislike of American family structures and then turned to me, the American parent in the room, and said, "I don't mean to say bad about English, because you English." These interrogations were occasionally awkward for Dan and me because we disagreed in one way or another with the American mainstream position (accurately) articulated by the students. But we remained a site to be interrogated, as the physical manifestation of Americanness within the space of the classroom.

This firm line that our students drew between Arab and American identities, norms, and customs obscured the fact that the discourse of ʿarabiya that they invoked is, in fact, an American discourse. Neither pan-Arabism nor the discourses of shared identity deployed between Arab migrants/refugees and host communities in Arab countries are identical in structure to the form of ʿarabiya detailed here. Instead, ʿarabiya forms the way it does because of the presence of a culturally dissimilar and dominant other to construct their communal identity against.

The work that 'arabiya does is also compatible with the patterns and expectations of ethnicity/panethnicity in American culture and politics and particularly the form that dominates in large, multicultural cities like New York: that coethnics will share meaning and practices with each other, that differences among members are not as important as the differences between them and the majority, and that they will work together in various ways. (The forms of 'arabiya that might be formed in France, with the broad anti-identitarian trends in social life, would necessarily be different.) The practical discourse through which the participants in activities at the AAA build 'arabiya is inevitably structured by its American context. The women in my classroom would not be 'arabi the same way elsewhere.

The way the students in my class created 'arabiya required that they understand themselves as other than American, even as the identity they created was deeply premised on being located in America. But while this form of identity worked well for them, it had its limitations, particularly in that it reinforced differences between Arab and non-Arab Americans. While 'arabiya helps build a community in ways that make it possible for people to understand themselves as sharing a common fate and enables political action to address that fate, it makes it more difficult for commonality to be found between different individuals. When might 'arabiya in this form not be a useful political identity construction, and what other forms of identity might work instead?

Second-Generation Identities

Suleikha, my friend and the youth program director at the AAA, and I sat in the side room upstairs at the AAA's offices. In the main room, the kids in the summer program were having lunch, and Suleikha was prepping for the afternoon craft: making Arab flags out of construction paper and then name tags for the kids to wear when they go out on field trips.

Suleikha called one of the younger kids in to talk with us. He was six or so, and she knew him from the tutoring program she ran during the school year. She asked him where he was from. "Louisiana," he said.

She tried again. "Where are your parents from?"

"All my parents are from Louisiana," he said.

"What country did they come from? What's your background?"

"'Arabi."

"Okay, what Arab country?"

"I went to an Arab country."

"Which one?"

"The first one."

"You mean the first one on a map? Morocco?" He agreed, but Suleikha was unconvinced; there are very few Moroccans living in Bay Ridge. She asked again, "Where are you from?"

"I'm from Allah," he said.

She burst out laughing, and said, "Yes, you're absolutely right. Go back to playing."

We finished setting up the name tags. Suleikha asked an older kid where the little one was from, and he responded without hesitating, "He's Palestinian." Somewhere along the way, the kids decided they wanted to play Seven Up and a game called Dead Fish that involved lying flat on the floor. We never got around to making those flags.

For the adult immigrants in my ESL classes, the creation of 'arabiya as a discourse makes a single community out of a huge wave of migration and becomes part of the daily lifeworld of practice the women inhabit. But their children, whether born in the United States or recently arrived with their parents, are differently placed to draw from 'arabi discourses. Much as their parents might want them to reproduce the discourse of 'arabiya perfectly and try to train them in it, the children end up finding spaces between a pure version of 'arabiya and a pure Americanness.

The summer program at the AAA was strongly and unsubtly intended as a pedagogical exercise in 'arabiya. The schedule for eight of the eighteen sessions involved an activity specifically geared toward teaching 'arabiya. Wednesdays were labeled "culture days," with a specific pattern of activities: an Arabic lesson in the morning, a music lesson or craft in the afternoon. In addition, two other craft days had Arab identity themes: a "collage day," with the theme of "expressing yourself," which could easily become a lesson about respecting one's Arab heritage, and making door hangers with each individual's name in Arabic. The marketing for the program highlighted "recreational, cultural and educational activities which in the past have included Arabic lessons, arts and crafts projects, Debke (traditional Arabic dance) lessons, and community service projects." The message being sent in the promotion and organizing of the program was that this was a space where Arab culture would be taught and Arab identity produced. This Arab identity was explicitly an ʿarabiya identity. Dabke, a Levantine dance, is presented as an "Arab" dance that is equally traditional for all children, and national origin differences were performed through activities, such as making the flags, that recognized difference while emphasizing that everyone held a common identity (having an Arab national origin).

The actual practice, however, was very different. I attended the first two of the "culture" days and found that the scheduled focus on Arab identity dissolved nearly immediately. Sara, who taught ESL with me, was available to teach Arabic only for the first few sessions. However, after teaching the students to write their names in their first class, she seemed to run out of lessons. She began her second class by saying "Sabah al-khair, kaif halkom?" (Good morning, how are you?) to try to get the students' attention. "We don't understand you," several of the older children said. "You don't understand me? Well, good morning," she said, without turning it into a moment to teach them these common Arabic phrases (which, probably, many of them knew already). She then said that they would color today, passed out papers, and made no effort to teach Arabic. The scheduled Arab music classes also failed to materialize, despite the fact that Suleikha had been playing phone tag with the friend of a friend for weeks before and during the program. After the program ended, I asked Suleikha, "Did you ever make *fannous ramadan*?" She explained these kids weren't really into arts and crafts, so they ended up canceling all the craft activities because it was most important to follow the children's desires, to make it a fun program for them.

The program's original shape was dictated by the impulses of the immigrant, parent generation: to take the notion of ʿarabiya that had been assembled by immigrant Arabs and to pass it on, in its entirety, to their children. But in the hands of the children's generation—which includes both the literal children who attended the program and Suleikha, who is the daughter of immigrants and was born and raised in Brooklyn—the practices of the space shifted sharply, away from the direct reproduction of ʿarabiya.

The 'Arabiya Dialectic

I often spent my time at the program sitting with the younger children. Suleikha and I were the only adults affiliated with the program, and we both had a maternal energy the younger children sometimes preferred, while the teenagers who were volunteering for the program got along better with the older children. One day at lunch, I was sitting with Mohammad, who was six years old, eating our sandwiches. His sandwich was baloney on potato bread. I pulled my hummus and arugula sandwich on multigrain bread out of my purse and began eating. "What sort of sandwich is that?" he asked.

"Hummus and lettuce," I said, deciding not to try to explain arugula.

"What's hummus?" he said. "I know what lettuce is."

I was momentarily shocked. "Hummus," I said in Arabic.[5] "Chickpeas. It's Arab food."

"I like all kinds of sandwiches," he said. "I like cream cheese sandwiches best." And he picked up his drawing of Optimus Prime to show it to me proudly.

On the one hand, this seems like a story of a totally assimilated child. But during a presentation by Sgt. Qudsi, an Arab American NYPD officer, on the first day of camp, he exclaimed excitedly that he was 'arabi and identified his three sisters by saying "that's [name], she's 'arabi too." Mohammad knew that being 'arabi was a socially relevant fact. But he was confused by my mentioning hummus; he liked baloney and cream cheese sandwiches, and he drew pictures of Transformers and was impressed that I recognized them.[6] Mohammad, like the rest of the children in this program, is already *both* Arab and American, and his experience of his world is structured by this identification.

Lunchtime was an excellent moment to witness this. Over the four sessions I saw, all the children routinely brought lunches, though at the first sessions several mothers, having not known to pack them, ran out to buy lunches from local stores. Usually the oldest child in the family distributed to their younger siblings the components of lunch from a single plastic grocery bag.[7] The contents of these lunches were about evenly split between Arab and American dishes: a large Tupperware of *koshary* shared between four cousins, *lahme* sandwiches on pita bread, or folded-over flatbread.[8] The rest were Lunchables, turkey and cheese sandwiches, slices of pizza, or bagels purchased by older cousins when the children forgot their lunch money. Even Arab main dishes were served with Oreos or Nutter Butters or potato chips on the side. Despite this diversity of lunches, there was no mocking about different categories of lunches, no trading of foods (though there was a commendable amount of sharing of cookies and crackers). It was all just lunch, and the kids ate what they had, shared with their siblings, and spilled their juice on the table with alarming frequency.

The way language was used in the camp also demonstrated this sort of easy transition between American and Arab. Many of the younger children referred to themselves as 'arabi (not Arab) at various times, suggesting that their ability to code switch was not yet highly developed. While Sgt. Qudsi was talking about traffic safety, one of the girls volunteered as an example of someone in *falasteen* (Palestine) who went out in the road and got hit. In another incident, three older boys had been horsing around and one of them, an inveterate joker, had grabbed ten dollars that had fallen out of another's pocket. "Give that back, it's my money," its original owner said. "No way, it's my money." "No it isn't, you're lying, give it back." "Come on, how're you gonna prove it's your money?" "*Wallah* [by God], it's my money!" the owner said. The joker returned it with a little huff ("Geez, don't get so upset"), but the invocation of *wallah* was enough both to secure that the money was actually the other child's and to make him feel obligated to return it. When Suleikha played Arabic pop music over speakers during free play time, in an attempt (as she told me later) "to get at least a little culture into them," at least one student came up to her and shyly asked if she had a specific song on her iPod. (She teased him for his taste, saying it was cheesy, but then went to look.)

In particular, Palestinian identity was a part of the landscape of the program, as it is generally at the AAA, in part because of the composition of its staff, in part because of the size and rhetorical dominance of the Palestinian community in Bay Ridge. During free drawing time, several of the boys repeatedly drew Palestinian flags, not always correctly. Children wore Palestine-themed necklaces, one had an IM name with the word "Palestine" in it, and several spoke of traveling to Palestine/falasteen to go visit. Many Palestinian Americans have stories of being told that Palestine doesn't exist or being unable to find it on a map in school as a child. Others note the experience of trying to talk about Palestine in public is met with awkwardness and discomfort, if not outright hostility. But at camp, Palestine was a real place, one that could be collectively talked about and used as a sign of identity, without anxiety.

Outsiders who came to visit the camp publicly referenced their ʿarabi identities or connections to Arab communities in order to locate themselves within the space. Sgt. Qudsi, for instance, met every instance of a child telling him his or her name with "Oh, I have a [relative] with that name," whether the relative was cousin, nephew or niece, or brother or sister.[9] When he was describing a potential abductor, he described him as wearing "one of those Muslim caps, a kufi" and that he was "a nice guy, an ʿarabi guy." Two representatives from the Brooklyn District Attorney's office, who held office hours at the center once a week, stopped by the camp and gave an impromptu presentation, distributing coloring books and talking effusively about how excellent jobs in city government were. (This was mostly lost on the six- and seven-year-olds in attendance.) The employee who did most of the talking was non-Arab. However, he was accompanied by the other DA's office employee, a white woman who married an Arab man, converted to Islam, wears hijab, and was at the AAA's offices regularly, interacting with children and adults. While she might be an unusual or marginal member of the Arab community, she possessed enough markers of ʿarabiya to help her be a part of the sense of the community as a whole.

The children in the program were the products of their parents' ʿarabi social milieu. They were raised in Arabic-speaking households, were exposed to Arab culture such as popular music and foodways, and were sufficiently embedded in the organizational structures of the community to be sent to the AAA's summer program rather than a non-Arab program. But their practice of ʿarabiya was much less interested in drawing sharp boundaries between ʿarabi and American. Instead, it built a dialectical relationship between the two to make a comfortable space for existing. Because of their youth, there was a great deal of fluidity in this boundary—one could have lahme one day and Lunchables the next, watch the Transformers movie devotedly and harbor an affection for cheesy Arabic pop music.

The ease of this fluidity may change as they get older. Both the boys and girls in this class may grow up to have a more difficult time code switching between the forms of 'arabiya and Americanness that may be demanded of them, publicly or privately. But at this juncture, they were able to take and subvert the demands made of them to publicly be Arab and be something else at the same time.

Conclusion

The concept of "Arab Americans" is often a misnomer. There are many Arab communities in the United States, shot through with differences based on national origin, time of immigration, class, education, and religion. For there to be meaningful political action that works under the banner of an Arab American identity, there needs to be a critical mass of individuals who feel tied to that identity and connected to others who share it. It is in the purportedly apolitical spaces of community service organizations and other institutions—shops, coffeehouses, places of worship—that people can develop this connection. The women who sat in ESL classes with me and the children who ran riot around me at lunchtime developed that connection in the spaces of the AAA, even though they likely did not set out to do so intentionally. The identities that are built across the table of 'aseed or Oreos are then internalized and practiced in ways that make it possible for the practitioners to use them as the basis of political claims.

The development of these identities can take place in almost any social space where people can participate alongside each other and come to recognize each other as belonging to the same community. It can happen intentionally or incidentally, or might even be contrary to the preferences of those who organized the space. But two things distinguish the AAA's spaces and suggest some specific outcomes of their spaces. First, there were very few participants or leaders in the programs of the AAA who weren't plausible candidates for membership in an Arab community. Most staff were ethnically Arab (and a number of the non-Arabs were Muslim in a majority-Muslim space). Teachers in the ESL program did not impose a strict hierarchy between themselves and the students and in several cases were Arab immigrants themselves. The outsiders who were present, such as myself and Dan, were viewed as collaborators, not authorities. By contrast, an ESL program that had mostly white American teachers who kept to a firm curriculum and gave formal assignments might have taught the students more English but might have involved less space for collective identity development and might also have become a space of discursive misrecognition or other forms of injustice against participants. (By contrast, both the director of adult education and the KGIA liaison at the AAFSC, in charge of important educational spaces that had potential to support and build community, were white women during my research, and the ESL teachers they employed were professionals who did not necessarily consider themselves as fellow community members with their students.) Collective identity building was central to the work the AAA's educational programs were doing, whereas in a different sort of program its formation might have been less explicit and less integrated into the process.

The second relevant fact about the AAA's practices is that the organization was willing to make the connection between collective identity and collective action. Participants in AAA programing were exhorted to register and vote once they became citizens and invited to demonstrations in favor of New York public schools having days off for Eid. Young people in particular were encouraged to volunteer and participate in community-focused activities. All participants in activities at the AAA were invited to make a connection between their commonly held identity and forms of change they wanted to see in the world. An organization could easily serve as a place for an Arab community in practice to be formed or a common identity to be developed, and not provide a bridge from that shared identity and community into forms of public action. Providing that bridge does not mean that an organization is political in the sense meant by US tax law where it distinguishes between nonpolitical tax-exempt organizations and taxable political ones, but it does provide more space for engaging in more open contestation, becoming a part of the political life of one's own time and place.

Regardless of how it is nourished or situated in the institutional contexts that support it, the concept of 'arabiya helps to create a living Arab American community out of the many people of Arab descent in Bay Ridge. Once that Arab community in practice has been constructed, those who identify themselves with it become bound to the organizations and institutions that help construct that identity. They can mobilize others using that identity and use that mobilization to accomplish things they believe are important, especially for people like them, or to turn toward outsiders with the steady knowledge that they have a community (constructed and articulated through the ʿarabiya framework) that they represent with members who stand behind them. But the existence of that community as well as the turn toward outsiders means that there are new sets of interlocutors to take into account and new possibilities for discursive misrecognition. In the next chapter, I examine how these factors influence the large number of young women who rise into leadership positions in Arab community institutions.

4

The Panopticon of Bay Ridge

Young Women as Community Leaders

To study the Arab immigrant community of Bay Ridge is to watch young Arab women. They're everywhere you look: in the offices of community organizations; at the forefront of political rallies; walking the streets or riding the subway in gossipy strands; dancing through crowds to riotous applause. For non-Arabs looking toward the Arab Muslim community of Bay Ridge, the position of women is an endless source of fascination. Are they forced to cover? Do their fathers and husbands oppress them? Are they allowed to be educated? When outsiders see them in roles of leadership, they want to know how the community feels about them as leaders, whether they have to break rules to hold those positions of power. Given the lack of information and prevalence of stereotypes about Arab culture and gender among most Americans, the high visibility of women as community leaders is a disruption to the expected pattern and requires interrogation.

This interrogation is a clear indicator of the role of stereotypes in limiting the interactions of outsiders with Arab American communities: the notion of the disempowered, oppressed/suppressed Arab Muslim woman and her patriarchal, dominating male relatives is so strong that its shadow dictates the questions and frames that outsiders see when they look toward Arab communities. Arab women are active participants in all parts of community life, and any understanding or analysis of Arab Americans that assumes they are silenced or passive is demonstrably incorrect. Before Arab American women speak, they are put into a position where they must defend themselves from those assumptions. And because gender roles and norms are one of the key ways that American culture understands itself as different from Arab culture, the women who take these leadership roles are particularly monitored by outside viewers who want to interrogate them. They are aware, at all times, that they are representatives of Arab America and responsible for combatting the discursive misrecognition of their communities.

This is clearly a form of panopticism, in the Foucauldian sense. The all-seeing eye of the disciplinary structure convinces you to conform yourself to its practices. The panopticon works as a technology of discursive misrecognition because of the way it compels both silence and forced speech on its inhabitants, who are forbidden from freely participating fully in an ongoing dialogue with others and may only remain silent or repeat prescribed sentiments dictated by the watchers. This is one of the functions of the panopticon: to constrain how those who are stuck within it can participate in ongoing practical discourses. (Of course, in the original prison panopticon, it was to remove them altogether.)

At the same time, there is an internal panopticism affecting Arab American women that does not involve discursive misrecognition. This panopticism, enforced through the community-wide disciplinary technology of gossip, demands that women adhere to traditional Arab gender roles (which are shared between Muslim and Christian Arabs). Deviations from these norms will be reported through the community (particularly to parents, for girls still living at home) and can have consequences for women's lives as participants in the community: inability to find marriage partners, difficulty finding work in community institutions, or social snubbing.

From the one side, Arab women are pushed into the spotlight in a response to discursive misrecognition and have to put on performances and provide accounts of themselves that will satisfy non-Arab interlocutors about their lives. At the same time, they are called upon to give accounts of themselves to the Arab community that show they publicly adhere to gender norms and practices, some of which non-Arab interlocutors would find disconcerting. Arab women must simultaneously meet the demands of two different panopticons, which are sometimes irreconcilable.

In this chapter, I take as assumed that women's autonomy and ability to be meaningful public actors do not require abandonment of minority cultural practices, even if some of those may be rooted in or have echoes of patriarchal or misogynist rhetoric.[1] That is to say, I believe quite firmly that advancement for women's issues, voices, and perspectives is compatible with a wide variety of cultural and social contexts *and* that they require substantive changes in all (or almost all) cultural and social contexts. Gender as a practice limits, defines, and shapes people's lives in every place where it appears. In the vast majority of those, it serves to restrict and limit the lives of women and of those who do not conform to its usually binary structure. (It also restricts and limits men's lives, but frequently in ways that confer privilege.) In this chapter I examine how women navigate civic and political action under conditions where their gender puts them at the center of different lines of political contestation and assumptions.

Where Are the Women? In Community Organizations

Women and girls were central to the functioning of community organizations throughout Arab New York.[2] At the AAA, women held key leadership roles. At the start of my fieldwork, the staff was five women and three men, and all of the women were Arabs from Bay Ridge; in 2012, the staff was seven women and three men, and three of those women had roots in Bay Ridge's Arab community.[3] In addition, Linda Sarsour, the organization's director, is quite possibly the most powerful political figure in Arab Bay Ridge. She is smart, well-spoken in both English and Arabic, and well connected, and has an impeccable sense of political timing. She commands the organizational resources to mobilize hundreds of volunteers for a community event or for a get-out-the-vote drive and has a platform for presenting her issues to any forum she wants. She also has the personal connections that make organizing in Arab American communities possible. As more than one of my informants said, Linda is the community's daughter.

In addition to women leading the AAA, its services focus particularly on women. The majority of the adults who walk through the center on a given day are women, participating in the ESL program, seeking assistance for things like welfare benefits, health insurance, and other household needs, or accompanying their children to the wide variety of children's programming. (As mentioned in chapter 2, Arab women have particularly low labor force participation, suggesting that their time is mainly focused on reproductive household labor.) There was also always, in my time studying the AAA, specific programming offered for girls, while there has never been any specifically offered for boys. In the fall of 2008, there was the Princess Club for elementary school students and Girl Talk for middle school and high school students. Those projects waned because of changing distributions of employee responsibilities, but in the fall of 2009 Brooklynat, a program for high school girls focused on community service and activism, began and was still running as of winter 2013. Najmat Falasteen (Stars of Palestine), a high school girls' dabke club, met at the center for the duration of my fieldwork, although it was not technically run by AAA. Outside of formal girl-specific programming, high school girls were frequent volunteers at the center and employed in the Summer Youth Employment Program (SYEP), alongside high school boys, and the tutoring and summer programs had roughly equivalent numbers of boys and girls.

Young women, usually Linda and the members of Najmat Falasteen, also serve to represent the organization in public. Najmat Falasteen performed at almost all the public-facing events of the AAA during my fieldwork. For instance, when the development director of the AAA came up to my ESL class to announce the clothing bazaar (a free clothing distribution event held in Sunset Park as a part of the national Arab American Day of Service), the first question that the women in the class asked him was whether there would be dabke. While Najmat Falasteen were performing at the bazaar, most of the Arab attendees sat on the steps of the recreation center where it was held and watched them, while other attendees continued picking out clothes. At the Arab American Bazaar, Najmat performed on the stage and later joined a women's dabke circle in the crowd along with other members of the community.

Young Arab women are equally visible in the forms of Palestine activism with their roots in Arab immigrant communities.[4] The crowds that attend Al-Awda's demonstrations and events are mixed gender and tend to include entire families, with husbands, wives, and children, often traveling with friends. Among both adults and youth, plenty are female, and they stand intermixed with and march alongside men. The real impression, however, is made from the dais. The most visible representative of Al-Awda is Lamis Deek, a young lawyer with offices in both Bay Ridge and Manhattan who usually served as MC for demonstrations and events. Like Linda, she is fluent not just in Arabic and English but also the language of social justice movements and solidarity alongside the language of Palestinian and revolutionary nationalism. But she is far from the only woman to speak for Al-Awda. Of the Arab-identified individuals who speak at Al-Awda events, whether from Al-Awda or other organizations, young women are sometimes the majority of speakers and never represent less than a third. Most of them are college students and speak about the commitment of youth in an way that is not gender marked, serving as the voice of what leaders in Al-Awda call "the generation of Gaza," those who got involved after the 2008 Israeli bombardment of Gaza. In addition, young women are a part of visual representations of the Palestinian movement, such as the color guard at an event (four young men and three young women) or those holding the sign at the front of a rally.

There is even room for fairly young girls in the practice of Palestine activism among immigrant families. I saw many children at Al-Awda marches and events, boys and girls, being socialized into the politics of the movement by their parents. After a long rally in December 2009 (an hour and a half of speeches, after a half-hour delay in getting started), we marched via a circuitous route from Times Square to the Israeli consulate on Second Avenue. While the rally had had a sound system, the march had only a few bullhorns. Given that the crowd was about a block long, it was impossible to hear what was being chanted at the front from the middle or the back, so we chanted in small pockets, led by those around us. Standing near to me was a girl, perhaps eight or nine years old. She was wearing a heavy parka, her hair in two braids sticking out from under her winter hat, marching with her father. In a loud voice, she was following the chants around her. Someone who had the bullhorn noticed her, and went over to her. He handed her the microphone and asked her to lead the chants for all of us. She pulled herself up proudly and began calling her chants into the microphone. Occasionally, when she chose one that was fairly radical (such as *bi ruh bi dam nifdiki ya falasteen* [with spirit, with blood, we sacrifice for you, oh Palestine]), her father would shush her and get her to shift back to another one, like "Free Free Palestine." When she eventually handed over the megaphone to someone else, another marcher, an older white man, came over to her and told her that she had a strong voice. Her father smiled, obviously proud.

Living in a Fishbowl

The young women who take on these leadership roles in the community are aware of the fact that they are being watched. I attended (and made cookies for) a bake sale held by the Brooklynat as part of a fund-raising effort for a breast cancer walkathon, their first project. At first I stood and chatted with the new youth coordinator and handed my infant son around to both girls and boys who wanted to hold and play with him. At a certain point, however, I noticed that I was not the only white woman in the room. The other two were also there to function as observers; one was a journalism student at Columbia, the other a recent graduate from a film program. The journalism student was covering the Bay Ridge beat, while the filmmaker was working on a film about young Arab American women. The journalism student talked briefly to some of the girls but seemed very reticent and didn't have concrete questions to ask. The filmmaker was a little more proactive, sitting down with some of the girls, explaining her project, and asking if they thought their parents would sign a release for them to be filmed at the second day of the bake sale. The girls agreed to take the releases home, and two or three mentioned that they had been interviewed in other documentaries. There was neither excitement nor anxiety about the prospect of being the subject of news attention. In fact, they seemed to expect it.

Many of the Brooklynat's projects seemed to be organized around the idea of visibility. Both the walkathon and the bake sale were chosen in part because they would make Brooklynat a group that would be *visible* in the broader community. And much of what happened during both that first day of the bake sale and the second, when we stood outside in the cold and sold to passersby, was about being seen and recognized. The mothers and kids who came through recognized the girls and their organization and praised the girls for their community service; so did the adult volunteers and visitors, Arab and non-Arab, and the few community members who passed by. A major part of the experience was the announcement of it, via Facebook, email, and posters. While the Brooklynat attempted to organize other events, they frequently fell through. The next major project that got buy-in from girls, volunteers, and community members was a mural-painting project, which was also framed to me as a chance for there to be a public, noticeable, visible sign of the Brooklynat's contribution to the community.

The level of media observation that was expected for these girls was a topic at the first Brooklynat meeting, which was largely led by two young Arab women on the AAA's staff, one a recent college graduate who moved to the city for school, the other a college student from the neighborhood. Both of them spoke of the importance of girls getting out there and representing the community: "they" don't think of Arab girls as leaders and have stereotypes of them as oppressed, so it's important that girls stand up for their community and be seen in public. The girls all nodded along, as if this was incredibly obvious. The staff members also spoke of the importance of media training because the imagined media interlocutors "might try to trip you up, try to get you to say something anti-Semitic or that they could cut to make you look bad." Media interaction was necessary and inevitable but ran the risk of being dangerous. Being watched had consequences, and therefore the girls had to be prepared and ready to enter into the conversation, to discipline themselves so that outsiders wouldn't come away with the wrong impression, which could have real consequences for the girls and their community.

This sense of outside observation was also something that Sarsour remarked upon in an interview with me, very early in my research. When I asked her about the benefits and costs of women being so prominent in community organizing, she responded, "I almost feel like it's okay that the non-Arabs see the women on the forefront. It brings down the myths and the stereotypes that we're disempowered, that we walk behind our men, and that sort of junk that people ask us. We're young women, we're covered, we're educated, we have children. [It makes] people look at us in a different way."[5] She also remarked upon how non-Arabs she's working with will comment with surprise that "they [husbands] let us out" or let them stay out at night or that the women they are talking to are educated.[6]

As Arab women go about their work keeping activist and service organizations going, they continually run up against stereotypical assumptions about Arab Americans. Arab gender norms are "understood" by outsiders in ways that require certain types of behaviors from these women in leadership positions: they must demonstrate that their lives are not what their interlocutors expect, regardless of what their own feelings are about gender norms in Arab communities. They also must prepare themselves to be constantly ready for these interrogations, just as the prisoner in the panopticon must always be waiting for the eye of the guard to fall on him. Their ability to find themselves fully recognized in dialogue with others is foreclosed by this requirement that they must always be ready to provide an accounting to stereotypes reinforced by those same others—and the hard truth that their accounting may not be accepted.

Internal Panopticism

Just as these women in leadership positions are being watched by non-Arabs, they are also the objects of a gaze directed at them from within the Arab American community. One of the many things that my informants repeated over and over again was that Bay Ridge was a village where everybody knew everybody. This sense of small community is enforced through gossip, both the telling of stories between individuals, especially women, about third parties and the reporting back to relevant authority figures, such as parents, of women's and girls' behavior. The gossip thus transmitted may be a fact, an observation, or a fabrication, but it generally involves pointing to unseemly behavior or publicly praising respectable behavior when it occurs.

Arab communities, both Muslim and Christian, have a particular set of norms for what constitutes proper female behavior. These do not correspond perfectly to the image of the suppressed Muslim woman, but they do reflect a set of norms that constrains women's autonomy, much as gender norms in most cultures do. Perhaps the most intense norm is that women, particularly unmarried women, should limit their contact with unrelated men. Interactions that are necessary for work, for community organizing, or for education are usually acceptable, but social interaction is seen as dangerous to women's virtue and propriety. Socializing in single-sex groups, and preferably in private spaces (such as homes), is seen as ideal and unimpeachable, and public socializing in mixed-sex groups is generally regarded as questionable. (Men also socialize in single-sex groups, either in public spaces or in private ones.) More permissive families would be comfortable with limited socializing between males and females, particularly in public, but might still forbid dating and romantic entanglements. Any sexual contact between unmarried persons is considered totally inappropriate, and women bear the greater burden of stigma for being sexually active outside of marriage.

In addition, unmarried women are supposed to live at home and be useful to their mothers in household labor, although generally the money they earn from working is considered theirs. Married women are supposed to have full responsibility for household labor and child raising, although, again, money they earn is supposed to be theirs. Education is prized for young women (and men), with a priority on staying close to home and earning degrees that have clear professional potential, but career is usually seen as secondary to marriage and family in women's lives, even after they have earned advanced degrees. Some marriages are arranged by families (usually with the approval of the spouses), and marriages that aren't arranged are usually subject to family approval; marrying without receiving parental approval would be scandalous.

Young women who deviate from these norms suffer reputational damage and concrete consequences for their deviation. A girl who is seen socializing with boys or staying out late in public will be "talked about," and her parents will likely be called to let them know that they should discipline her. A wedding that is not approved by the family will not be attended by community members, and the couple may be socially shunned. Women who don't adhere to the cultural conventions of what young Arab women should be will be socially stigmatized, and their actions will be bring shame upon them and upon their families, unless their families repudiate them.

This sort of community surveillance of people's actions also fits the model of panopticonic power that Foucault describes. In the panopticonic situation, you are fundamentally *known*, in your truest being, by your ever-observed behavior. This requires a constant biographical examination of everyone to ensure that they are in conformity and determine their position within the system.[7] There is also threat of punishment for deviations from what one should be; "the whole infinite domain of the nonconforming is punishable."[8] The exercise of panopticonic power creates a field of knowledge, and knowledge of a subject then works to create a field of power to control that subject.[9]

The world of gossip and self-monitoring that is Arab Bay Ridge is such a world of panopticonic surveillance, a world where the biographical examination of the subject produces normalized subjects that conform to the rules and principles set out for them and know the disciplinary risks of deviating. The knowledge created through community surveillance and spread through gossip both constitutes and is the product of a form of power: to know someone is to have the power to influence the individual's status and prospects in the community, and to hold power over someone is to have access to a piece of knowledge about the person that might be either beneficial or detrimental.

It is worth pausing to unpack the different panopticonic conditions created by the gaze of non-Arab interlocutors and the Arab community. When the conditions of the panopticonic gaze combine with a high concentration of stereotypes, assumptions, and false impressions about the subject at the center of the panopticon, as happens when non-Arabs are panopticonically observing Arab women in leadership positions, the result is that the observer acquires no new knowledge about the subject at the center. Instead, the panopticonic exchange usually helps reinforce the preexisting ideas that the observer has of the subject. The subject has, under these conditions, the opportunity to ignore or dismiss the observer or to behave in ways that only on the surface respond to the observer's demands. But where the panopticonic mechanism is used by those who do have access to intimate knowledge of the subject, the field of knowledge that is produced is different. It runs the risk of producing knowledge that the subject, or the other interlocutors, might consider truer or might incur more specific punishments for nonconformity. I bring up this difference because of a phenomenon I noticed: the same women who could dismiss the assumptions and interrogations of non-Arabs about Arab norms of gender as unimportant or obviously misinformed would, at the same time, take seriously the way they were interrogated or pressured to perform for Arab American audiences. The knowledge that was produced within Arab spaces was more disciplining—because it was understood as having consequences in spheres that actually mattered to the women subjected to it or because it felt "truer" to their self-understanding. Not all panopticons are created equal, though their fundamental mechanism is the same.

At the same time as young women who are leaders in their communities find themselves to be under constant interrogation by external observers, in frameworks riddled with discursive misrecognition, they are also located in the panopticon of Bay Ridge, where they can be punished for deviation from an elaborate network of social norms. In their experiences of living at the center of their communities, they are equally subject to both of these forces, which collectively circumscribe their lives.

The Micropolitics of Internal and External Panopticism

That external and internal forms of panopticism interact in the lives of young Arab women in leadership positions does not mean the interaction takes a single standard form. In fact, its forms are incredibly variable, depending on where the interaction happens, who participates in it, and what are the most relevant forms of meaning, identity, and gender practices at that moment. In order to understand the processes at work in this interaction, we cannot look for macro-level processes but must instead turn to the microanalysis of how people, individually or communally, wrestle with these issues.

To engage in this microanalysis, I present five separate stories of places where external and internal panopticism interact in the life of young Arab women who are deeply implicated in institutionalized community structures. Two of these are public or semipublic conversations and interactions I witnessed as participant-observer during my fieldwork; three of them are the stories of individual women I knew and interviewed specifically about their experiences with gender and gossip (the common name by which internal panopticism goes among the women I knew). Through tracing the lines of power and positioning against these processes, I lay out both the ways that panopticism is deeply embedded in women's experience of political and community engagement and how they analyze and cope with it.

Pleasing One's Mother

During a down moment of AAA's summer program, two sisters who were SYEP staff were hanging out in a side room at the office with me, Suleikha, and a few other of the SYEP kids. The younger sister, Rania, was fourteen, a member of the dabke troupe, and aggressive and unsubtle in a very teenage way. (Over the course of the program, her younger brother, a camper, once burst into tears, saying she had scratched his eye. Her response was that, no, she had called him ugly, and she had no *idea* who had scratched his eye.) Rania was talking about the upcoming dabke performance and expressing an adolescent world-weariness about it. "My mother is always so excited that I do dabke," she complained. "When she's with her friends, she'll always tell them that I do dabke, and then her friends will ask me to dance. So I totally go off on her about it." Suleikha suggested that Rania's mother just wanted to brag about her. Rania shrugged: "She can't brag about me much." Then she turned to her sixteen-year-old sister, Inji. "I mean, with you, she can at least say, oh, my daughter wears the hijab." Inji looked very hurt by this and challenged her sister: "She doesn't do that, she doesn't say that about me." Rania seemed a little embarrassed to have upset her sister, and said, "Well, she does it about me all the time."

There is a profound awareness on Rania's part of being observed and of how she is represented in her mother's speech. Her mother needs positive examples of Rania's behavior to share with her friends. Although I did not know Rania well, she presented herself as a social butterfly whose priorities were friends and fun, not obedience or respect or academic success. But her mother has to be able to talk about her with her friends and to emphasize something that gives Rania a good reputation and reflects positively on her own parenting. Dabke provides that opportunity. Rania is able to be talked about positively because she is a reproducer of the Palestinian cultural heritage, someone who is called upon to perform (literally) in front of others. Her skill at this socially important task is a credit to her and to her parents.

What Rania recognizes and Inji pushes back against is that Inji's hijab also makes her a credit to her parents. Inji is the quieter of the sisters. While not shy per se, she is less aggressive and outspoken than her sister and a little more serious in demeanor. From Inji's response, it seems as if she views her own covering as an individualist action—perhaps a form of personal piety, a gesture of her relationship to God and the Muslim community, or her interpretation of religious principles. She wants to maintain this reading of her action. What makes her uncomfortable in Rania's statement is that her personal choice has a profound social meaning. Many young women in Bay Ridge do not cover. Those who do are more likely to be students at a religious high school (Inji and Rania attend the local public school), who are required to do so as part of their school uniforms. However, their immigrant mothers nearly universally cover, and many wear jilbabs rather than Western clothes.[10] Wearing hijab, like dancing dabke, makes a girl a credit to her family and is a major plus in her reputation. While Inji may not wear the hijab because she wants to please her parents, *doing so does please them.*

This act of pleasing her parents constitutes a valuable piece of information to enter into the panopticonic field; both Rania and Inji are "proper" subjects of that panopticon, though in different ways. The biographical examination that must happen with both of them—and which inevitably happens in any social gathering of community members—is something they can both pass, though in different ways. Rania made Inji uncomfortable here by acknowledging the fact of that examination, but they are both subject to it, regardless of whether or not they choose to recognize it. Despite the fact that they are subject to this disciplining vision that asks them to be proper Arab girls, they still deviate from the narrative that discursive misrecognition would assign to them. Both have active (if single-sex) social lives, are regular volunteers at the AAA during the summer and the school year, and seem to feel, given Rania and Inji's constructions of their selves, that they are able to make their own choices for their own reasons, whether it is to cover or to dance dabke. The fact of panopticonic observation does not mean that either girl is lacking in autonomy. Instead, they have the ability to navigate within the constraints of disciplinary surveillance and figure out how they should respond to its demands.

Hayy Mish MSA

In December 2008, the Break the Siege on Gaza Coalition, organized by Al-Awda with other Arab and Muslim groups, held an event at City College, obviously run by City College students with outside assistance, on different religious perspectives on the situation of Palestine.[11] I arrived a little early and spent a few minutes going through the metal detector and having my bag searched. This is the only Palestine activist event I've ever been at to have these security precautions, but similar events held in CUNY facilities tend to have such measures. A group of young women, dressed in hijab and jilbab, were clustered around one of the auditorium doors, chatting in Arabic. When I walked toward the other door, they corrected me: this is the women's entrance. This was the only event I've attended in Arab New York to be gender segregated. Even other events that might have been strict about division were more flexible: at the first Brooklynat meeting, a boy (someone's younger brother) who was sitting in the lobby doing his homework asked, "If this is a girls' meeting, do I have to leave?" and was reassured that he could stay since he wasn't bothering anybody. Men also taught women's ESL classes without problem.

As I entered, it was unclear to me if the women's section was the back of the auditorium or the right side, as not very many people had arrived yet. I sat in the back right, where most of the women attendees were clustered. At the front of the room, a young Arab woman who did not cover was standing near the podium, helping set up for the panel along with several young Arab men. A few non-Arab women entered. When they walked toward the front, one of the covered women stopped them and said, "This is the ladies' section." They sat, slightly confused. Eventually, a white woman in a flowered dress headed down the steps. The designated usher stopped her, saying, "This is the ladies' section." The white women said, "There are transgendered people, you can't make that distinction." Awkwardly, the usher said, "Well, physically, you're a woman, and women sit here." "You're making that assumption by looking at me, there are intersexed people in the world." "Please, just sit here." "Isn't this a public event?" By this point, the other women in hijab were calling the usher's name, trying to get her attention. The uncovered woman organizer came up the stairs to join the argument, which was mostly carried out in Arabic.

The white woman was given permission to go sit in the front, but the argument continued past that point. Eventually, the unveiled woman said sharply, "The first word they think when they see us, sexist. *Halas* [Enough]." She stormed up the stairs. The conversations continued. A few minutes later, I heard someone say, "*Hayy mish* MSA [This is not the MSA, Muslim Students' Association]." And then, a few minutes later, "You come into a space, you have to be able to follow its rules." I was unsure if she was talking about the American university space or a Palestinian cultural space. Further attempts by women to cross into the men's sections were stopped by the usher, though each time there was an outcry of her name that carried the unmistakable aura of "leave it alone."

The male panelists arrived, half an hour late, which is practically on time in Arab community activism. A young man introduced the event and thanked their cosponsors, "our brothers in the MSA and our sisters in Women in Islam." While the panelists spoke, the veiled women around me were on their computers, IMing friends, taking the occasional note. Men who came in late sat in the back left of the auditorium. No one told them to move. The unveiled organizer came up to the women's section, handed out cards for the Q&A, and sat down next to another uncovered Arab woman to try to recruit her for their student organization. It sounded like she was having luck.

The woman in the flowered dress was convinced that she knew what it meant to have a gender-segregated event: it was an unjust imposition of a binary division between individuals that she felt was both morally unsupportable and factually incorrect. The question "Isn't this a public event?" is a direct act of pushback to the notion of a "community space" that the gender segregation created: Arabs could *not* make manifest their gender norms in this space because they were fundamentally counter to a universal mode of publicness that the woman, as a member of a broader liberal society, had a right to demand. Arab cultural norms were fundamentally suppressive (to her and, I would guess, to others) and could not be permitted to be articulated.

Her reaction constitutes a fundamental misunderstanding of the function of gender segregation in Arab, and non-Arab Muslim, community spaces. The male/female divide is used not (only or always) to suppress women's voices but to create separate spheres of proper behavior, wherein men and women can function freely. For people who follow conservative Muslim principles about gender relations, being in a mixed-sex group is substantively more suppressive than being in separate groups; men and women would have to be scrupulously correct in not touching or, in some cases, looking at each other to remain within the sphere of appropriate behavior.[12] While the woman in the dress's interrogation about transgender and intersex individuals has merit, Arab cultural norms, like American ones, are deeply binary in their gender division and deal with gender-variant individuals by assimilating them to one of the existing gender categories.

From the outsider's perspective, the gender segregation of this space constitutes an injustice. But from the perspective of the young women (and men) who enforced it, it constituted a response to internal panopticism. Young Muslim women organize in a separate group, apart from the young men, in order to have their own space for religious and community work, and their group was cited as a cosponsor, indicating that it is acknowledged as a leader within campus Muslim circles. Their decision to maintain gender segregation at the event (when an event hosted only by the Palestinian students' group might not have been segregated) has two clear possible justifications. The first might have been that there were women who attended the event who would have been profoundly uncomfortable mixing with men, for reasons of religious propriety, which places restrictions on men and women's looking at each other in public. Frequently, when muhajjabat are asked why they cover, usually their second answer (after that God requires Muslim women to do so) is that they don't want men looking at their bodies, that this makes them feel exploited. So, it is entirely possible that a subset of the religious women involved in planning this event would have felt uncomfortable if they had not had a women's-only space to occupy at the event—or that religious men involved in the planning would have been uncomfortable if they had had to share space with women.

But another real possibility is that women planning the event were thinking not about their own discomfort but about the broader social consequences of being seen mixing with men. The crucial word here is "seen"; young women know they are being observed by the panopticonic power of the community, whether in the form of adults or other young people, male or female.[13] This event took place in the evening, on a weeknight. City College does not have a large population of students who live on campus, and all the Arab American young people from the outer boroughs I know who attend college in New York live with their parents while in school. (Some young people probably also live with spouses.) This means that the young women who attended had to secure parental permission to be out until ten o'clock at night, perhaps longer if they lived in Brooklyn or Queens. (There are small Arab communities in Upper Manhattan, but it's impossible to tell where these students lived.) Frankly, there are many non-Arab parents who would be skeptical of such an endeavor in New York City. But given the emphasis on reputation and the fact that coming home late at night is one possible way to become the target of gossip within the community, attending this event probably involved a negotiation about its respectability. Being able to say to your parents that the event would be gender-segregated, that you would not be sitting with or interacting with boys while attending it, is an important way to justify the acceptability of staying out, as is the fact that it was a lecture on Palestine, a perennially legitimate topic of political engagement in Arab communities. For some, the gender segregation may have been morally important. For others, it may have been strategically important.

The women who implemented the gender segregation did so for reasons that were wholly comprehensible to them. But when confronted with the objections of the woman in the flowered dress (which were formed by the context of discursive misrecognition), they immediately began to figure out how, concretely, to respond. Their initial reaction was to try to maintain their preferences, but when that produced conflict, they permitted deviations. In the end, their conversation revolved around how strict to be and how to respond. The conversation took into account both the context of discursive misrecognition ("the first word they think, sexist") and the importance of maintaining their own position in the face of that misrecognition ("you have to follow its rules"). The flexible response that developed—allowing men to sit on the far left back, allowing the woman who wanted to go to the front to go there— was a response to the context of misrecognition, which allowed the internal panopticon to be satisfied (those young women who were subject to it maintained their propriety), while avoiding direct confrontation with narratives of misrecognition.

Intimate Misrecognitions: Rose's Boyfriend

The first time I really spoke to Rose was after the first Brooklynat meeting, though we had met before. She sat next to me, still in her school uniform of black jilbab and white hijab, and we chatted pleasantly before the meeting began. When Suleikha arrived, Rose moved to stand, knowing we were friends, but Suleikha motioned her to stay, and sat kitty-corner from us. After the meeting, Rose and Suleikha had some sort of exchange—which might have just been a series of looks— and then Suleikha mentioned that I was here, as "another intellectual," someone for Rose to tell about her problem. I put on my best impartial-observer face and nodded, said I'd be happy to provide an opinion. Nervously, she agreed, seeming both eager to talk and apprehensive. I followed them back to the office Suleikha shared with another staff member. She locked the door, and Rose sat with her back to it, "because I might need to run away," she said.

She proceeded to tell me about her boyfriend. "I don't even know why he's my boyfriend," she said. "He just said he was on IM. I don't know why I went along with it." He wasn't a classmate from the Muslim school she attended or a Muslim at all, just someone who knew a friend of hers, who didn't even live in the neighborhood. Since they had started "dating," he'd been pushing all of her boundaries. He scrolled through her phone, found pictures of her uncovered, and asked her to take more and send them to him. (She showed me them: posed in front of a mirror, making duck face.) He asked her to write his name on a part of her body and take a picture of it to send him. He wrote suggestive IMs and text messages about how he knew she wanted him. This came to a head recently when, while sitting in the park together, he leaned over her and kissed her. "It was like he raped my mouth," she said, simultaneously ashamed and pleased to be venting. "When I imagined my first kiss, I always thought it would be with my husband on my wedding night. Truth." Apparently her displeasure at the kiss led him to break up with her over text message, but then text again two days later trying to arrange for them to get together. She was trying to decide what to do.

I was supportive and said in no uncertain terms that the guy was a putz, that the best thing to do was just cut off all contact—block him on IM and Facebook, don't answer his calls, just never see him again, since he wasn't someone she had to see. Without being too didactic—I hoped—I tried to affirm her experience that yes, the transgression of boundaries that she'd experienced was wrong and was not her fault. I avoided using the terms "sexual harassment," "sexual assault," and "enthusiastic consent," though I was certainly thinking them.[14]

A few minutes later she left the room to take a phone call. Suleikha and I spoke of high school boys past, dismissively. "Yeah, well, I found a way around that," I snarked. Suleikha, who had met my wife, rolled her eyes. "That doesn't work so well for the rest of us."

That evening, Rose friended me on Facebook. For the next year, I followed her status updates: new bands discovered, silly posts with friends, student government announcements, the success of the new (coed) debate team.

A year later, on a hot August afternoon, I walked across Bay Ridge to Rose's house to interview her about her experience as a young female leader. Her house, a large, single-family detached home, was deeper into

Bay Ridge than I'd ever had cause to go, past the central Arab business district and down close to the water. I rang the bell and she answered the door, opening it just slightly. This was, I realized as I stepped into the blissful air conditioning, the first time I'd ever seen her uncovered; she was wearing just a T-shirt, jeans, and a nice everyday pair of gold hoop earrings. She apologized for the mess; her mother was out of the country visiting relatives and none of her family members were keeping up with the housework. She poured me a glass of cranberry juice, and we sat down at the dining room table.

"It's good," she said, when I described the fall class I was teaching on gender and politics in the Middle East, "that you're doing it. I mean, because you're someone who knows Arab people, who spends a lot of time down here. I think a lot of people try to talk about things who don't know what's actually going on. But you're someone who gets it."

She spoke passionately about the lack of community spirit and leadership within the Arab community. "Too many people don't do anything," she said. "It's great that we've got all this support from people of all religions and races, and we need it, but five Arabs could do more than a hundred white people, you know?" The Arabs need to step up. She thought the younger generations were doing more of the necessary work and the older generation was standing in the way of change. At the same time, she was blasé about the importance of women's leadership in the community: "Let the men lead. It's all they're good at. The women are going to actually get the work done."

Being a Muslim, she said, was her primary identity. Being Arab was second, but it wasn't even close; she was a Muslim first. Her first relationship was to God, her second was with her parents, and she wanted to please them, in that order. She was comfortable with conservative gender roles: she spoke of getting married soon and said that women shouldn't take high political office, both because of the inappropriate level of scrutiny it would place them under and because of their familial duties.

I asked about the effects of gossip in the community. "People will talk if you do anything," she said, rolling her eyes. "If you're seen with a boy, or whatever. My parents got calls about me walking around on the streets with some of the boys from debate. It's hypocritical, because the people calling your parents up are always the ones whose kids are misbehaving the most." "So what do you do about it?" I asked. "I talk to my parents," she said. "It's corny, but I believe that telling them the truth is the best thing to do." She also thought that the level of community surveillance has its benefits; if a potential mother-in-law is scandalized by her hanging out with the boys from the debate team, that's not a family she wants to marry into. It's also a reminder, she said, to make sure that you're behaving appropriately because someone is watching. She spoke about never going out of the house looking like a slob because it's important to always appear put-together, of watching her public behavior because someone will notice if she misbehaves. "It's good to be encouraged to be one's best," she said.

I didn't ask about it, but she brought up dating on her own. "I used to think dating was okay if you didn't do anything wrong," she said, looking away. "But then, I mean, I had some experiences. It's too hard to guarantee that nothing inappropriate is going to happen. So, yeah, I've sworn off dating. It's not worth it."

We talked about the college application process. She wanted to be a civil engineer and was applying to a bunch of colleges all over the East Coast. At the time, her top choice school was Sarah Lawrence. I mentioned that my wife's alma mater, Smith, both is a women's college (she liked that Sarah Lawrence is so largely female) and has a big engineering program. She was curious. "And, you know, if it's a really good school my parents would probably let me live on campus," she said, before she caught herself. "Oh. It's in Massachusetts. Duh. I couldn't commute there. I'd have to live on campus." And she laughed.[15]

In dating the guy in the first story, Rose was breaking the rules, the (frequently spoken) cultural consensus that Arab girls, particularly but not only Muslim ones, don't date, certainly not in their teens and usually not ever. But Rose's boyfriend wasn't just a way for her to resist expectations and rules. He was also a palpable manifestation of non-Arab narratives of what Arab women are, of the particularly nasty Orientalist sort. The desire to see her uncovered, the compulsion to know what exists under the scarf, the nagging, nearly violent desire to reveal her as harem girl fantasy: these are some of the darkest sides of American and Western cravings imposed on the figure of the Arab Muslim woman. In breaking up with him, Rose reclaimed her right to self-definition and found a way to break away from a particular concrete manifestation of fetishizing Orientalism.

In giving up dating altogether, Rose was not giving in to internal panopticism, choosing to follow its rules unthinkingly. Her relationships with the boys on the debate team were more substantial than her relationship with the terrible boyfriend because they involved spending time together in public, both in the school context and socially. This was, in fact, *more* of a deviation from convention because it was unconcealed.

That Rose felt that many of the panopticon's demands—that men and women have separate yet mutually supportive roles in life, that women should have primary concern for family and children, and that an arranged (or at least family-brokered) marriage at a young age is a reasonable social practice—are legitimate does not mean that she was not engaging in acts of resistance against this system. In fact, buying into many of the rules of the discourse was a major part of her resistance. In choosing to do things that potentially get her gossiped about, like spending time with boys and taking on leadership roles at her school, she ended up using the community's own rules to justify her behavior. "Nothing inappropriate" was happening when she walked around the neighborhood with the guys from the debate team, and she was able to claim this because she knew and agreed with community notions about what counts as inappropriate behavior. Although Rose remained deeply tied to community norms and practices, she had space, in her public person, to transform the components of her life that seemed most necessary. Although her public avowal of norms that non-Arab, non–Muslim Americans might find odd could seem to be a confirmation of the misrecognized narrative of the oppressed Muslim woman, her leadership and her ability to resist are predicated on it.

I Don't Have Family Here: Iman

"You know who you should talk to," the current youth coordinator at the AAA said to me when we sat down to chat about the Brooklynat. "You should talk to Iman. She's taking over when I leave for grad school this fall, and she's from the neighborhood. She'll have things to talk about with you." I nodded and let her introduce me to Iman, a twenty-year-old college student wearing a plain yellow hijab, jeans, a long-sleeved T-shirt, and a cardigan sweater.

When we got a chance to sit down together a few weeks later, Iman was slow to warm up to the interview. As we started to talk about her background in community organizing (working with the Muslim American Society, a Muslim youth organization) and her plans for Brooklynat, she kept glancing down at my notebook. I put my pen down and kept talking. Whether it was the fact that I stopped taking notes or merely that she had grown accustomed to talking to me, the conversation began to go more smoothly.

Iman was intensely critical of the ways in which girls in the community limit themselves in their goals. Part of her goal for Brooklynat was to help the girls in the group start to think more broadly about their goals and to possibly think about college in terms of their own desires, rather than as an automatic, doesn't-matter next step. What the girls need, she said, is the strength to speak up, to ask for what they want. The problem is less about parental refusal and more about the question never being asked in the first place. "It's not like their parents will beat them or something, or even really say no," she said, shaking her head. "They just need the strength to insist." She used the common metaphor of Bay Ridge as a small village but emphasized its dark side. "Some people just never leave," and their worldviews and expectations are limited and constrained because of it.

I asked her how she came to have this critical stance. The answer came in the form of an autobiography. Her mother was uneducated, was married at fifteen, and had seven children, not uncommon in Yemen or among Yemeni immigrants in New York. More surprising was that she successfully left her abusive husband when her children were young, which impressed upon Iman the necessity of women's financial independence. She taught her daughters that they must have their own careers, even when married, because they can't take their husband's support for granted. Iman had been working since she was in high school and paying rent since she was fourteen.

She called out the hypocrisy surrounding gender roles in her community. "It's much stricter for girls than for boys," she said. "Boys can do whatever and nobody's going to stop them. My oldest brother, he's got a baby, and he never sees her, or her mom. And my mom still lets him live at home. Like, if I did anything like that, she'd never talk to me again." In high school, there were people who couldn't hang out with her because of her "family situation," or because she was seen out walking on the streets late at night. "Which is because I'm at work or school! It's ridiculous. I just ignore it," she said, rolling her eyes. "I don't care."

Her mother was conscious of the reputational effects of Iman's actions and tried to get her to change. "She worries when I want to do things," Iman said. "So whenever there's something I want to do, to go somewhere or stay late or maybe overnight to a conference or something, I have to think really hard about whether it's worth it, and whether I want to go enough so that it'll be worth arguing with her about it. So sometimes I don't go, or sometimes I lie about what I'm doing, just to make it easier." A major source of arguments over the past few years has been the question of going to the movies. Her mother has the impression, mainly from American television, that movie theaters are a space for inappropriate sexual activity among teenagers. (For conservative Arab Muslims, premarital kissing, or almost any kissing in public, would count as inappropriate sexual activity. Handholding would be frowned upon, as would merely having a boyfriend or girlfriend.) Iman explained that she kept having to tell her mother, "All you do there is watch the movie! I'm going with friends! It's fine! I kept telling her she should just go with me, to see what it's like." Although her mother never took her up on this, she eventually relented, or at least quit trying to stop Iman from going.

Iman knew that her reputation had been damaged, both by her "family situation" and because of her own independence and actions, though she presented herself as unconcerned about it. Elsewhere in her narrative, those consequences appeared; neither her sister nor her cousins married Yemenis, which would have been socially expected. One married a Palestinian, another a Pakistani, and another a Dominican, who wasn't even Muslim. "People wanted to go to the wedding," she said, "but they were like, who are these people?" When I asked her, now five years older than her mother was when she married, if she was under pressure to get married soon, she shrugged, a little relieved, and said, "No, I'm not, because I don't have any family here."

Iman could not meet the demands of Arab community panopticism; she simply lacked the ability to be disciplined into a proper position. Even if she wanted to conform in all relevant ways, her "family situation"—a very delicate way of saying the scandal of her mother publicly revealing her husband's abuse and leaving him rather than allowing it to continue—would continue to plague her in terms of community status. She might be able to overcome it, but it would require a scrupulous sort of conservatism and probably a rejection of her mother's actions, which it was clear she did not want. She had already been judged, and all of her actions, wherever they were observed, added to her preexisting reputation.

But to Iman this meant liberation more than loss. She might not have been able to marry a Yemeni, but she would also get to choose her own marriage partner, seemingly without constraint (given the variety of marriage partners her sister and cousins had chosen) and on her own timeline. She might have been the target of gossip when she walked home from the subway late at night (where late might mean nine or ten o'clock), but she also had the freedom to build the community organizing skills and work history that would serve her professionally. She got to go to the movies, no matter what her mother's anxieties. She had made herself free to critique the system, by accepting the distance she had already been set at from it, and then taking more distance.

At the same time, she was not leaving the observational orbit of the Arab American community. At the time of our interview, she still lived with her mother, wore the hijab, and worked at the AAA, after having been involved in the Muslim American Society. Each of these kept her further from the discursive misrecognition of the non-Arab community and kept her within the sphere of Arab panopticism. Since then, she has stopped covering and worked first for a social service organization that serves Muslim women and then for the public school system. She lives apart from her family, having moved in with a non-Arab boyfriend who became a husband, and has had her first child. She can be powerfully critical of her own community—a recent Facebook status argued that Muslim fathers do more to screw up their daughters than anyone else—but she maintains her deep membership in it. By spending so much of her youth working in the Arab Muslim community, she managed to not have to provide accounts of herself to those who might misrecognize her, but her preexisting, and inevitable, loss of reputation means that she is free to voice her dissent without additional cost.

There Are Rules: Suleikha

Suleikha is the closest friend I made in the course of my fieldwork. Her position as youth education coordinator at the AAA meant that she was a necessary contact for me in the early stages of the research. The office she shared with the adult education coordinator was where I would sit and chat before and after teaching English. Suleikha is about my age, was in graduate school while we worked together, and shares my affection for sci-fi television. We got along well and soon were actual friends, not just fieldwork acquaintances.

The irony of this is that Suleikha is also the perfect "key informant" from an ethnographic point of view. Born in Brooklyn and living from her teen years on in Bay Ridge, she has an insider's deep knowledge of the community. She is fluent in Arabic and English and volunteered at the AAA for over a year before she took an AmeriCorps position there. Like the textbook key informant, Suleikha had a critical distance from the Arab community of Bay Ridge. In her childhood, she had lived in a less heavily Arab neighborhood and her social circle was never all, or even majority, Arab. Her Egyptian identity was as strong as her Arab identity, or stronger, but she also strongly identifies as American and, in particular, as a Brooklynite.

Throughout the time I've known her, Suleikha has been fierce in her criticism of the Arab community, particularly its insularity and the ways in which debate can be stifled by the priority placed on harmony. Frequently, she is more critical than I am, in part because she is more closely bound to these constraints than I. Her time at the AAA ended poorly because of her strident disagreement with people in leadership positions around particular practices. A cloud of gossip and poor reputation stuck to her, which has nagged her professional development since. After her time at the AAA, she spent some time volunteering with the American MidEast Leadership Network's nascent community services program in Astoria, but her involvement was generally kept quiet so as to avoid reputational repercussions within the community. She has since worked for other organizations in the Arab American community as well as at other jobs and for city political campaigns.

Suleikha doesn't care whom she pisses off; she knows when she's right, and she's unwilling to compromise in explaining why that's so. Her willingness to be critical, her disgruntled attitude, and her deep knowledge of the community made her a critical asset for my fieldwork. I am also pleased to call her my friend.

I interviewed Suleikha on a chilly fall afternoon in Park Slope. She was at the tail end of a photo shoot with a mutual friend of ours, focusing on fashion and identity. She seemed awkward and nervous, but posed and tried to chat. A male friend of hers (who was non-Arab and non-Muslim) tagged along. (They started dating shortly thereafter but have since broken up.) After the shoot, we all went out to a small Egyptian restaurant Suleikha knew and had a quick lunch. Then Suleikha, her friend, and I went into the coffee shop next door so we could talk.

I told her I wanted to write about the experience of gossip in the lives of young women in Bay Ridge, and she was immediately enthusiastic. "It's just awful," she said. She made allusions to the problems at the end of her time at the AAA, a story we'd talked about many times. But she also pointed back to experiences she had in high school. At one point, another girl in her grade called up her parents and said that she had a boyfriend. The boy in question was a friend of Suleikha's, and she spent time with him socially, but they weren't dating or even interested in each other. But Suleikha knew that the girl who made the call actually did have a boyfriend. "I could have called up her parents and gotten her in trouble. But I didn't, because that's just not right."

The photo shoot she had just done had been about fashion, and she had, uncomfortably, talked during it about her transition away from hijab. Until shortly before I knew her, she had covered. Although she is vague when she speaks about it, her Facebook photos show her wearing an encompassing and loose hijab throughout college, along with skirts and baggy shirts, and then transitioning to covering just her hair, but not her neck, and still wearing loose clothing, before ceasing to cover her hair altogether. She still wears skirts all the time, and I've only occasionally seen her in a shirt with less than elbow-length sleeves, but neither covers her hair nor wears high-collared shirts.

She spoke, during our conversation, about why she "de-hijabed," as she put it: she was tired of the system of expectations demanded of her as a muhajjaba. She wasn't supposed to talk with boys, was supposed to be demure and reserved in public, was supposed to always be an upstanding representative of what an Arab or Muslim girl should be.

More than just covering, she had to only dress in certain colors, certain patterns, certain shapes. "I didn't want to be like that," she said, so she stopped. I couldn't help but agree: the image of a demure and retiring Suleikha seemed absurd.

She shook her head and sipped her mocha. "That's what I don't get, all these girls who wear hijab but with, like, regular clothes, or who hang out with boys or whatever. That's not how they're supposed to act." I pushed back: isn't it possible that there are lots of ways to cover and that wearing a scarf over your hair doesn't have to come with the full set of restrictions? She was emphatic that the answer is no. "There are rules, there are things that are expected of you," she said.

Eventually the conversation moved on to marriage. She had had several guys interested in her when she was younger but never anyone she actually wanted to marry. "Do you think you want to get married someday?" I asked, hoping that this wasn't putting her friend in an awkward position. "Sure," she said. "If I find someone. But I don't care if it's an Egyptian or a Muslim or anything. It just needs to be the right guy."

Suleikha might seem to be a perfect confirmation of the narrative of female suppression and liberation that marks mainstream discourse about Arab Muslim women: excluded from the community for being too outspoken, breaking away from restrictive dress codes, seeking a universal exit. And yet Suleikha's story could also be used to push back against those same discursive misrecognitions. While some members of the borough Arab communities didn't want to interact with her because of her stances (or perhaps merely the outspoken way she stated them), others were perfectly comfortable working with her. When she covered, she was just as outspoken as when she didn't; she simply felt pressure to be otherwise. When she uncovered, she was still able to be a part of community organizing efforts. Her story is much more complicated than any misrecognition narrative that someone might want to impose on it.

Suleikha was a clear-eyed evaluator of the conditions of internal panopticism that Arab American girls and women experience in Bay Ridge. Understanding that her life choices were severely constrained by the way the eternally watching eye of the community would judge her behavior, demeanor, and choices, she decided that the wiser choice of action was to step away from it. But Suleikha's understanding of the community's rules was conservative, even more so than Rose or Iman. While they looked for ways to carve out space from the rules or obey them at the edges while enjoying the benefits of their means of exception to them, they understood the role of surveillance within the community as conditional, able to be evaded, argued with, or obeyed only partially. Suleikha admitted of none of this; there *are* ways muhajjabat should act. And when she stopped wanting to follow those rules, she had to stop following the dress code. For Suleikha, there is no means to resistance except escape. The only thing you can do is bust out of the panopticon.

Conclusion

On the first day of the Brooklynat bake sale, as the reporter and the filmmaker milled around looking for data and I passed my baby between girls and boys who wanted to play with him (and took the opportunity of having my hands free of baby to eat cupcakes), I noticed how incredibly comfortable all the girls were in the lobby of the AAA, a space that existed at the limits between public and private. Mothers with small children walked through on their way to tutoring upstairs, volunteers and friends of the organization stopped by and congratulated them, and everyone passing through bought a cookie.

As the bake sale ran down, several of the Brooklynat who were also in the dabke troupe set up a pair of cheap computer speakers and one of their iPods and cued up some dabke music.[16] They began rehearsing informally for the next day's practice, starting and stopping songs, laughing and talking as they danced. Some other girls who were not a part of the troupe joined in, asking the more skilled dancers to keep it basic and even to teach them some of the more complicated moves. They danced and danced, and those who didn't watched, and talked, and ate even more cupcakes.

These girls owned the room that day. They had no anxiety about engaging in their lives in public space, and no one suggested that they dance later or in another location. The meaning of a room full of girls, filling the space with their music, their dancing, their cookies, and their voices, is clear: they know that they belong in a place where people are watching them and that they have the right to be there. These are not the invisible suppressed women of Orientalist discursive misrecognition; neither were they, in that moment, being demanded to provide an account of themselves to the panopticonic forces around them. No one asked them if their fathers knew where they were. Those girls were able to make room for themselves in community spaces and to put themselves in a position to be able to make their own negotiations with the multiple demands made on them from outside, and inside, the community. The ability to find spaces where discursive misrecognition is not entirely in practice and where accounts of the self can be temporarily put aside is necessary for all those who exist under panopticonic conditions.

Everyone needs a cupcake every now and then.

PART III

Everyday Identities

5

From the East River to the Sea

Organizing for Palestine

For many Arab Americans, being involved with the cause of Palestine is synonymous with political activism. Just as the actions of Israel and the need for a solution for Palestinians are perennial topics in Middle Eastern political circles, action focused on Palestine is omnipresent in Arab American communities, whether mobilizing to send financial support to hometowns or the needy in Palestine, petitioning the US government to change its policies toward Israel, Palestine, and Palestinians, or building networks with other, non-Arab activists in the United States and elsewhere to try to change public opinion on the conflict.

This is a challenge because the positions taken by many Arab (and a significant number of non-Arab) pro-Palestine activists are fundamentally different from those held by most Americans as well as the consensus among political elites about what constitutes a reasonable solution to the conflict. Among both left- and right-leaning Americans, the majority support a two-state, negotiated solution to the conflict. Most white Americans' emotional loyalties lie with Israelis, with whom they feel more cultural kinship than with Arab Palestinians. Most people prioritize a narrative where there is fault on both sides and what is needed is compromise and cooperation in order to bring peace.[1] But many pro-Palestine groups with roots in Arab communities as well as a smaller number of other activists disagree with this position. Like the two groups I study in this chapter, they support a single state on the territory of Israel/Palestine. They also engage in tactics that make non–Arab Americans uncomfortable or upset their conceptualization of the conflict. The most prominent of these at this moment in time is the Boycott, Divestment, and Sanctions movement, which calls for a boycott of Israeli goods and cultural production, divestment from Israeli companies, companies that profit from the occupation, and/or companies that operate in Israeli settlements, and economic and political sanctions against Israel until the occupation is over. In this narrative, blame is asymmetric (though many are critical of Palestinian political leadership) and rests in the hands of the Israelis; political pressure is necessary to force Israel to change course and support the eventual victory of a free Palestine.

The result of this gap is that pro-Palestine activism, particularly when carried out by Arab Americans, is rarely well received by nonparticipants and is frequently subject to continued discursive misrecognition. Organizations that voice these positions and those who participate in them are understood to be (inherently) hateful, anti-Semitic supporters of violence. In many cases, all Palestinians, or even all Arabs, are assumed to have these traits, unless they have actively demonstrated their allegiance to the American mainstream discourse. Regardless of what they actually say, think, or do, they are ruled irrational and irrelevant to the conversation—completely outside the any possible practical dialogue. Only those who agree on the first principles of the mainstream narrative are allowed to participate.

It is necessary to say that I believe that these assumptions that delegitimize Arab advocates for Palestine are unfounded in many cases. There are some within these movements who are anti-Semitic, as there are, unfortunately, too many anti-Semites among Americans of all ethnicities, and particular strains of anti-Semitism circulate in the Arab world and in its diasporas. Many who identify personally with Palestinians living under occupation, through family connections or other affective ties, may be very angry, which may be misread as hate by outside interlocutors. And there are different perspectives among pro-Palestine activists on the utility and legitimacy of violence as used by an occupied people against their occupier—an old question of *jus in bello*, just conduct of war. But by understanding all Arab pro-Palestine activists as violent, hate-filled, and anti-Semitic, their interlocutors cut off the ability to see the diversity within the community of those who support Palestinians as well as the basis of their beliefs and arguments. This prevents all of us from being able to engage with pro-Palestine activists, limits their ability to express their positions in public, and often consigns them to marginality and silence.

How do Arab-led organizations that mobilize for Palestine deal with the difficulty of advocacy under these conditions? To answer this question, I studied two very different pro-Palestine organizations, both of which were active and had a significant number of Arab leaders and participants. One, Al-Awda NY: The Palestine Right to Return Coalition, draws large crowds from the recent immigrant communities of Bay Ridge, Bensonhurst, and New Jersey to regular street protests, which include chanting in Arabic and invocation of Palestinian nationalist symbolism. The other, Adalah-NY: The New York Campaign for the Boycott of Israel, organizes small-scale performative protest campaigns against Israeli-owned businesses and Israeli cultural institutions and is organized by Arab, Jewish, and other professionals, both born abroad and in the United States.

In this chapter, I argue that the ways that identities are used, evoked, and developed within both groups constitute responses to the problems of trying to advocate for Palestine, particularly as Arab-identified people and organizations. Identity work within movements is a central part of the nexus between everyday politics and the conventionally political because identities are developed in micropolitical exchanges among group members and in the relationship between broad political discourses and people's subjective experiences of them, and then serve to structure how groups act and how they are received by interlocutors. As members of groups develop understandings of their individual identities and articulate collective identities that describe the communities they understand themselves as coming from or representing, or the nature of the group's internal identity, they respond to the political conditions in which their movements operate and help determine how their organizations will act in the public sphere.

Al-Awda: Building and Bonding a Shared Community

Despite the fact that Al-Awda is a public actor and carries out its actions on a public stage, the practice of identity it enacts is profoundly inwardly directed. To participate in Al-Awda's actions requires that the participants understand themselves either as a part of a unified, integrated Palestinian (secondarily Arab or Muslim) community or as engaged in supporting it. Their deployment of Palestinian nationalist symbols, their engagement in a discourse of resistance, and their assumption of a uniformly held Palestinian/Arab Muslim identity builds what Manuel

Castells calls a "communal heaven," protecting their political engagement from the discursive misrecognition that inevitably awaits it outside their walls.

Nationalism

Al-Awda distributes the same protest sign at all of its demonstrations. On one side appears their logo, on the other an image specific to the topic of the protest. The logo is densely packed with symbols. It depicts a fist, raised in struggle, against a map, clutching a key. The Arabic text *al-'awda* is written across the wrist.

The raised fist is a sign that dates back at least to the black power movement and is used by revolutionary movements worldwide. The map behind the fist depicts what is usually called "historic Palestine," meaning the territory ruled as Palestine under the British mandate, which is roughly contiguous with what is now known as the state of Israel and the Palestinian territories. Historic Palestine is rendered in the colors and pattern of the Palestinian national flag. The symbolism is not subtle.

The fist clutches a large key. This is a reference to the departure of Palestinians from their homes during the 1948 war between the nascent state of Israel and its neighboring states, who objected to the terms of its formation. Many Palestinians left their homes, because of direct violence by representatives of the emergent Israeli state, because of fear of that violence, or because they were anxious about the situation. Most of those who left believed that they would be able to return to their homes within a few weeks and, in general, brought few of their belongings, including their house keys. However, those whose homes were in Israel at the end of the war were not allowed to return and were never compensated for their land or possessions. The key here symbolizes this dispossession. *Al-'awda*, "return," references the "right of return," or the right of Palestinian refugees to move back to the homes from which they were displaced.

The text beneath the image reads "Free Palestine from the River to the Sea." The river in question is the Jordan, the sea the Mediterranean. "From the river to the sea" is a common way of referencing "historic Palestine" with easy geographical markers. It is also remarkably easy to

Figure 5.1. Author's photo from an Al-Awda protest on December 27, 2009, taken outside the Israeli consulate on Second Avenue in Manhattan. In the center is the Al-Awda logo; the other posters of similar size were made by the International Action Center.

rhyme in English, as in the frequent chant "From the river to the sea / Palestine will be free." By referring to all this territory as Palestine, the sign makes a clear statement against the legitimacy of the state of Israel. Palestine needs to be free, and it isn't because it is Israel.

This sign is a central part of the deployment of Palestinian nationalist symbolism within Al-Awda's actions. Its deployment of Palestinian national colors, an image of "historic Palestine," the key with its specific references to the Palestinian history of displacement, and its use of an Arabic word closely tied to specific demands of Palestinian refugee communities are all part of the performance of national identity, and nationalist claims, within the demonstrations.

Throughout Al-Awda's demonstrations and actions, similar national symbols and performances are repeated. For instance, the *kuffiyeh* or *hatta*, a traditional checked scarf, is worn by many participants. The kuffiyeh is worn in different styles and colors throughout the Levant and Gulf. In the West, from at least the 1980s, the kuffiyeh has been read as a mark of radical politics or pro-Palestinian political affiliation.[2] In the early 2000s, the pattern moved into the American cultural mainstream, and kuffiyehs were sold in generic apparel stores, stripped of much of their original meaning. (Urban Outfitters, for instance, briefly marketed the kuffiyeh as an "antiwar scarf," before it was pulled due to protest.) At Al-Awda demonstrations, two varieties of kuffiyeh are commonly worn. The first is the traditional square kuffiyeh, which consists of an embroidered patterned cloth with knotted fringe. Most activists wear it as a neck scarf, and women occasionally wear it draped around the shoulders as a shawl. At demonstrations, it is commonly worn by older Arab men, but not older Arab women; in the Middle East, the kuffi-yeh is traditionally a men's head covering (particularly worn outdoors), which may explain why more traditional women do not wear it. Some young Arab American activist women, particularly those that make up the "generation of Gaza," wear it also (as do young female activists in the Middle East). Both male and female non-Arabs wear it as well, with some frequency.

The other form is the narrow, scarf-type kuffiyeh. This consists of a long rectangle of kuffiyeh-print cloth with a political slogan and graphic (usually the Dome of the Rock or a map of historic Palestine) printed at the bottom, followed by the Palestinian national colors and some fringe. These kuffiyehs are significantly cheaper to produce than traditional embroidered kuffiyehs and are handed out at Al-Awda demonstrations. These are commonly worn by many different types of demonstrators, including Arab women of all ages, some Arab men (though more of them have traditional kuffiyehs), and non-Arabs. Whereas the tradi-tional kuffiyeh is frequently worn in nondemonstration contexts, the narrow kuffiyeh is really appropriate only for a protest because of the set of nationalist affiliations it carries in addition to its print: the slogan, the image, the colors of the Palestinian flag.

In addition, the Palestinian flag and references to it are everywhere at these demonstrations, not only on kuffiyehs. Physical flags on cardboard poles are distributed for waving and collected at the end of the demon-stration. The color scheme of the official signage, and even the clothing of the leaders of the demonstration and many of the attendees, is limited

Figure 5.2. Author's photo from the May 31 protest of the Israeli action against the Gaza Freedom Flotilla, organized by Al-Awda. In the foreground, the young men in the center and to the right are wearing triangular kuffiyehs; the woman visible between their shoulders is wearing a scarf-style kuffiyeh. Note also the Palestinian flag on the shirt of the young man in the center as well as the one being carried by a person in front of him.

to red, green, and black, and flag accessories are a frequent style choice. In addition to distributing kuffiyehs, people also walk through the demonstration distributing small tokens bearing the colors of the flag, such as key chains or cloth wristbands. T-shirts printed by activist groups tend to stick to this color scheme as well. There is also a habit that some of the young members of Al-Awda have of wearing the Palestinian flag draped down their backs like a cape, with the corners of the end with the black triangle tied around their necks. (I heard one member mention that his mother would be scandalized to see him wearing the flag like that, though he didn't have any reservations about doing it.)

The centrality of nationalist imagery was made extremely clear at an event held in honor of George Galloway, a British member of Parliament from Scotland who is outspoken in support of Palestine, on January 31,

2010, in Bay Ridge. Galloway was on a speaking tour, freshly returned from being ejected from Egypt and declared persona non grata because of his involvement with the Viva Palestina organization and its attempt to get humanitarian goods into Gaza and was raising money for the Freedom Flotilla.[3] The event was entirely framed in Palestinian nationalist symbols. Widdi Hall, where it was held, is usually used as a reception hall, particularly for community organization events and weddings. The room was set up for a lecture, and on the back wall a Palestinian flag had been hung. The event formally began with the MC asking us to rise for the Palestinian national anthem.[4] As the recorded anthem played, a color guard entered, with five college-aged members of Al-Awda each carrying a Palestinian flag on a cardboard pole. They all wore black shirts reading falasteen/Palestine in green print and scarf kuffiyehs around their necks. They stood at attention at the front of the room until the anthem was over and we sat; they then filed off stage.

The next two hours, until Galloway took the stage, featured speeches, films, and poetry in both Arabic and English. The MC explicitly stated that the goals of the organizations hosting, Al-Awda and the American Muslim Federation for Palestine, included an "uncompromised" Palestinian government and a free state of Palestine from the river to the sea, with Jerusalem as its capital. When it was time for Galloway to enter, he did so preceded by the color guard, dressed in all black with a narrow kuffiyeh around his neck, followed by a collection of notable men from Bay Ridge's Arab community.

Palestinian nationalism is not window dressing in Al-Awda's actions; it is central to how it performs itself, whether demonstrating for a crowd in Times Square or preaching to the converted at an event like the Galloway speech. It is not merely that the signs and symbols of Palestinian nationalism are permitted at Al-Awda's actions. Rather, they are actively spread through participants, through handing participants a scarf kuffiyeh, a Palestinian flag, a sign with a fist raised in struggle across historic Palestine and the word "return" written on the wrist. These symbols orient the organization toward an Arab identification and also mark out a distance between participants and mainstream American discourses around the conflict. It is this combination of identity differentiation and discursive distance that makes it more likely that Al-Awda participants may experience discursive misrecognition as they try to articulate their political goals. But at the same time, it powerfully reaffirms the legitimacy of these signs and symbols within the community that contains the organization. Here, at least, members may freely invoke these symbols and do so knowing that they have a community that recognizes them and affirms their use.

Resistance

Resistance is frequently interpreted by outside observers of Palestinian politics to mean "armed resistance," of the sort carried out by groups like Hamas or the Al-Aqsa Martyrs' Brigade. When participants in Al-Awda's demonstrations chant that "Resistance is justified / when people are occupied" or "Palestine is under attack / What do we do? We help fight back," interlocutors assume that these protesters are calling for violence against Israel, including Israeli civilians. When they hear the chant "Intifada, intifada, long live the intifada," they think of suicide bombings, armed gunmen, and rockets fired out of Gaza.

However, for most within Palestinian communities and those who spend significant time in them, little distinction is drawn between armed resistance and nonviolent resistance, what Omar Barghouti calls "civil resistance."[5] For instance, the first intifada in particular combined elements of military resistance, economic boycotts, general strikes, refusal to deal with the Israeli court system, demonstrations, refusal to leave one's land, and symbolic resistance actions like throwing stones, constructing barricades, and burning tires and flags. The notion of "intifada" includes all these actions, and to invoke it is to invoke the generalized sense of resistance, which means anything that Palestinians do to try to oppose the occupation.

Al-Awda frequently draws on this broader meaning of resistance and centers resistance as a concept in all of their demonstrations. The large sign carried at the front of Al-Awda marches reads "Resistance, Liberation, and Return by Any Means Necessary," a reference to Malcolm X's famous speech at the 1964 Organization of Afro-American Unity Founding Rally. Other signs manufactured by the group also specifically invoke resistance: "Palestinians Are Freedom Fighters," "Long Live Resistance in Gaza," "Tel Aviv Built On, Bathed in Blood; Long Live the Palestinian Resistance."

Speeches repeatedly invoke the term and its corollaries. They may simply praise "our beautiful resistance," as the MC said at the demonstration commemorating the one-year anniversary of the 2008 bombardment of Gaza, or describe Gaza as "the land of resistance and dignity," as a speaker from an allied organization, the International Action Center, did at the George Galloway event. They might also note the differences between the discourse of resistance they are using and the one used by interlocutors: "We are not confused," said a speaker from the International Action Center. "We know the difference between resistance and terrorism. We know who the real terrorists are," which was met with cheers from the crowd. They may make reference to discourses of *sumud*, as when a speaker at the George Galloway event said "for Palestinians, existence is resistance" (a slogan that is also the name of a pro-Palestinian cultural arts group).[6] They may even argue, as all three speakers did at an interfaith event at City College, that the Palestinian people have a legitimate right of defense and that Palestinian violence against the Israeli occupation is the moral equivalent of trying to force robbers out of one's house.

Resistance is also a critical part of movement self-representation and presentation. At the George Galloway event, two short films were screened. The first, played during the hour between the announced starting time and the actual beginning of the program, was a video called "I Resist," produced by a group called "Like Never Before." The two names are meant to be read together: "I resist like never before." The video featured a strong musical soundtrack, images from Palestine, and interspersed text that gave a series of reasons for resisting. The other short film, called *24 Hour Visa*, documented the Viva Palestina convoy, in particular the struggles and internal discord of the members, their difficult journey to Gaza and negotiation with the Egyptian authorities to be allowed in, and then the devastation they saw while in Gaza. (The majority of the film's time focused on the first two elements.) The film ended with the words, "Resistance comes in many forms. Telling this story is one of them."

The centrality of resistance ties Al-Awda to other social movements, particularly black nationalist and radical movements. Representatives of black radical movements are frequent speakers at Al-Awda events and draw on their own discursive vocabularies to build linkages between

Palestinian liberation and black liberation. Speakers at the Viva Palestina kickoff invoked the spirit of Harriet Tubman and John Brown, framed the question of Palestine as a question of empire and colonial oppression, and spoke of meeting in support of "all of brothers and sisters in the world." The event was held in the House of the Lord Church, a black Pentecostal church whose pastor, Herbert Daughtry, is well known for his work in CORE and other black movement organizations and was attended by Charles Barron, a New York City Council member and a former Black Panther. There is a history of ideological linkage here that goes back to the 1970s, and includes critiques of Zionism as racism and colonialism, critiques of Israel as collaborating with South Africa, and critiques identifying the conditions of Palestinians with the apartheid system of South Africa.[7] Black radical groups are not the only potential allies that draw on the narrative of resistance. Speakers from multiracial socialist groups, such as the International Action Center, Revolution Books, and NYC Labor Against the War, also draw on this narrative. This puts the use of the Malcolm X quote in a new light: not just borrowing a useful piece of language, but a meaningful engagement with a prior movement with whom members of Al-Awda find commonality.

The use of resistance by Al-Awda brings together these two strands of revolutionary and radical thought, both the widely disseminated frames of black and third world socialist rhetoric from the 1970s onward and the Palestinian resistance vocabularies of sumud and intifada as well as the rejection of the discourse of "terrorism" as a synonym for Palestinian political action. In many ways, this represents a coalitional response to the problem of discursive misrecognition. Black and other nonwhite articulators of third world socialist positions face the dual hit of making arguments directly contrary to fundamental assumptions by most Americans of how the world works while having marked identities. Like the Arab and Palestinian members of Al-Awda, they know that their analysis will be dismissed as soon as they start speaking. These two political discourses share some categories of analysis, and their articulators have a shared experience of failure to be allowed into practical discourses. By speaking with each other, they can both find an interlocutor who will not dismiss them without engagement and even find constructive agreement. For both black and Arab radicals, articulating these positions sets them further away from the mainstream conversation. But given both the inability of most Arab Americans to gain any access to that conversation and the limits and failures of the conversation to meaningfully change the circumstances of many black Americans, the strength gained from working with fellow radicals may seem like a worthwhile trade-off.

Palestinian, Arab, and Muslim Identities in Al-Awda

As I mentioned above, Al-Awda draws nearly all of its members and people who attend at demonstrations from recently immigrated Arab communities. Whether this is cause or effect, it is also true that Palestinian identity, or a pan-Arab identity tied to the Palestinian cause, is the assumed central basis of Al-Awda's work. Speakers invoke their own Palestinian identities repeatedly during events. A poet, performing at the George Galloway event, said in her introductory remarks, "People ask me, why do I always talk about Palestine? It is more than my blood, it is more than where I come from." A leader spoke about entering Gaza and feeling as if for the first time she were being pulled into Palestine, rather than being pushed out by Israeli soldiers, which was her experience of visiting the West Bank or her parents' hometown, which is within the borders of Israel. A Lebanese American college student began her speech by talking about how, since she grew up in a Lebanese family, she knew the basics of the struggle in Palestine, but that when she joined the demonstrations for Gaza it was the first time she really started to want justice for her people. Before the Viva Palestina convoy, she "had only gone to Palestine in my dreams."

There is an assumption that attenders at Al-Awda demonstrations speak Arabic or are familiar with it. Arabic music or untranslated clips from Arabic media are played at demonstrations or events, and some individuals speak Arabic from the dais. This was particularly true at the George Galloway event, where about half the speeches were in Arabic and where the MC tried to excuse the lateness of the events' starting by saying, "This is an Arab neighborhood, so." Every Al-Awda demonstration features chanting in Arabic, usually led from the dais but sometimes arising from the crowd. The most common is "bi ruh, bi dam nafdiki ya falasteen" (with blood and spirit we sacrifice for you, oh Palestine), a standard nationalist chant used in different forms across the Arab world;

"ya ghazza" (oh Gaza) is sometimes substituted for "ya falasteen" at Gaza-focused events. Other Arabic chants used during demonstrations invoke "yom al-'ard" (Land Day, a major nationalist holiday) or call for "falasteen hurriyya, falasteen 'arabiya" (Free Palestine, Arab Palestine). At one demonstration, the MC announced that the last chant was "bi ruh, bi dam," because she had heard complaints that there hadn't been enough chanting in Arabic—a suggestion that, for at least some in attendance, cementing an Arab identity to be shared among members or promoting the importance of Arabness in public was more important than chants that could be easily interpreted by passersby.

At Al-Awda events, when "the Palestinian people" or "the people of Gaza" are invoked, they are always figured as a single, undivided unit. A Palestinian priest at the George Galloway event used his speech to "send a message" via Galloway to the people and government of the United Kingdom, in the name of "we Palestinians—not Christians or Muslims, or the West Bank or Gaza, or Fayyad or Hanniyah. I'm talking about Palestine from the river to the sea, the melting pot Palestinians, no Muslims, Christians, Hamas, or Fatah, just united Palestine. We are ready to die for our cause." This was met with thunderous applause. The Lebanese American college student recounted a conversation with a person in Gaza who said that Gazans were totally unified: "When one is crying, we all cry. When one is sick, we are all waiting for him to get better. When one is attacked, we are all attacked." The people of Gaza, in particular, were continually invoked as steadfast, united, resisting, honorable in spite of their suffering.

While these descriptions were flattering, they lacked complexity. Rather than being individuals with political perspectives, Palestinians or Gazans are flattened into a unified mass, speaking only to assert their oneness. Palestinians still in Palestine are never given names or social histories. They exist only to be invoked, never to be spoken with. The tremendous diversity of opinion among Palestinians, which is a major factor in contemporary Palestinian politics, disappears on this view, to be replaced by an idealized unified people who exist as the foundation for the organization's politics, not as independent actors.

A similar flattening happens in the conflation of Palestinian and Arab identity. In chapter 3, we saw how processes of interaction among different Arabic-speaking immigrants created a shared notion of 'arabi identity that helped assemble a community out of individuals. In some ways, Al-Awda's actions assume that such an identity has already been identified, such that other Arabs are natural constituents for a pro-Palestine movement. But the movement from that assumption to assuming that Palestinianness is identical with Arabness erases the diversity of participants in 'arabiya, which is one of its central features. While many other Arabs are interested and enthusiastic about participating in pro-Palestinian activism, this form of rhetorical dominance within an 'arabi framework has the possibility to lead to fractures, resentment, or other disruptions within the panethnic identity.

A similar flattening takes place with regard to religion: just as Arab identity is dominated by Palestinian identity, so too does Muslim identity come to take center stage. This happens in a variety of ways at events, such as by talking about Palestine as Muslim land, inviting imams to give *da'awah* (pray) at events, while priests give speeches without praying, the invocation of Muslim phrases in the speeches made by members, such as calling for *takbir* and beginning speeches with the *bismillah*, and the explicit Muslim identity of allied groups.[8] The first follow-up demonstration for the Gaza Flotilla protests, for instance, was called in the name of the "Arab and Muslim community of New York and New Jersey."

New York's Arab communities, even the recently immigrated portions, are not universally Muslim, and New York's Muslim communities, like Muslim communities across the United States, are not majority Arab.[9] But this assumption of common ground between Muslim and Palestinian identity is an active part of Al-Awda's political practice. This may be the result of a conscious attempt to draw in non–Arab Muslims and Arab Muslims whose primary political identity is as Muslims, an effect of coalition-building with Muslim-identified organizations or individuals, or a set of "natural" assumptions that certain forms of cultural or religious practice can be generally understood and read by the people they anticipate will be at their events. But in each case, it demonstrates a form of turning inward, of solidifying a shared identity through repetition and reinforcement.

In fact, Al-Awda's actions, whether in invoking a Palestinian national imaginary, presenting a unified and cohesive Palestinian community (to which participants are assumed to belong), or using a vocabulary of resistance and struggle, generally are directed toward the creation and reinforcement of a Palestinian (or Palestinian-adjacent) political identity for participants and the organization as a whole. The organization's work emphasizes valorizing and supporting these identifications over attempts to communicate their principles or points to the unconvinced. Flyers, signs, even speeches given at non-Al-Awda events all leaned heavily toward repeating these gestures, rather than trying to bridge the gap between people who hold those identities and understand those vocabularies and those who do not. This builds a sense of community, a validation of identities, and a feeling of strength, which can be shared in particular by the Arab Americans who are most likely to be left out of conversations—Arabic speakers, immigrants, those whose language and frameworks for politics can't find a space in American discourses. They can find a haven for their voices within the organization that is hard to find elsewhere.

Adalah-NY: Connecting for Concrete Change

Adalah-NY's differences from Al-Awda are many, at the levels of membership, organization, and activities. But its identity practices are particularly different from Al-Awda's and show a different orientation toward insiders and outsiders. Members are organized around a notion of solidarity that presumes differences and prioritizes following the lead of those closest to a political conflict. At the same time, the group prioritizes a framework of strategy and concrete gains and the means by which they can be achieved. Although members would name their eventual goal as the end of Israeli oppression of Palestinians, the goals they focus on are concrete and limited in scope: to put a particular investor in settlements out of business, to convince a multinational corporation to stop selling technology to the Israeli military, to convince people to stop purchasing a particular Israeli-owned brand. But all of them require that the organization make an effort to convince those who are not already convinced to take a certain action, which requires framing and positioning their work to communicate with outsiders. These two facets of the organization synchronize to create a set of practices where participants' performances of identity are used strategically (as well as in principled ways) to communicate with nonparticipants, and where the frames they use for their work are oriented around ideas like solidarity and justice, which can resonate with a larger audience than Al-Awda's frames of resistance and nationalism. While Adalah-NY has not been able to achieve its end goals, it has had intermittent success in being allowed into more mainstream conversations—which provides both opportunities for practical discourse and more opportunities for discursive misrecognition.

Solidarity

The first Adalah-NY gathering I attended was an "open meeting," designed to introduce new members to the organization's work and ethics and bring them up to speed on current organizing. These meetings served both as an orientation and as a means of increasing the barriers that infiltrators from pro-Israel organizations would face in trying to get on the group's internal mailing list or gain advance knowledge about events.[10] One of the major features of the meeting was a conversation listed on the agenda as "Palestine Solidarity Activism: What Does It Mean to You?" Both potential members and existing members went around the room and shared their answers to the question.

It quickly became clear that there were two categories of answers being given. One category was a response to the question "what should a pro-Palestinian/pro-peace movement do?" The other was a response to "what is a solidarity movement in support of Palestinians?" A diverse group of individuals gave answers to the first question, which often centered around particular tactics and educational strategies to change the minds of Americans. But all the existing Adalah-NY members, and a number of new attenders who had previous experience in a particular subset of Palestine or other activism, gave very closely connected answers that highlighted concepts both of identity (being Americans, Jews, or diasporic Palestinians) and of being led by Palestinians still living within Israel/Palestine.[11]

The particular notion of solidarity used in Adalah-NY's work, and in other organizations in pro-Palestine and other movements, relies on two different principles.[12] The first is the notion that movements should be guided by those most affected by a particular issue. Rather than outside experts determining the structure and nature of a movement or explaining what proper solutions to the problems might be, solidarity discourse presumes that those who are actually living the problems have the best understanding of what the necessary actions are. The voices, analyses, and priorities provided by groups who hold this position (of being most affected) are taken as primary.

The second is a focus on the difference and distance between a member of the movement and the groups or people with whom they are in solidarity. Persons who are in solidarity with a group are not members of it. The positions they hold will be different. Palestinians who have immigrated to the United States, for instance, have a different experience than US-born Palestinians or other Arabs, and Jews or other non–Arab Americans have a different relationship still. But all members' relationships mark them as different from those whom they want to support. When they engage in political action, they must turn to those who are most affected and find ways to acknowledge their difference from them and work in concrete ways to allow them to meet their goals.

At moments when Adalah-NY has specific engagements with outsiders, beyond protests, this discourse of solidarity is central to their behavior. At the open meeting, beyond the discussion about what a solidarity movement was, the focus was on the call from Palestinian civil society for the global boycotting, divestment, and sanctioning of Israel, specifically embodied in the BDS document, meaning the 2005 Palestinian Civil Society Call for Boycott, Divestment, and Sanctions. The BDS call is a collective statement signed by over 150 Palestinian organizations, including political parties, charities and NGOs, and activist groups from the West Bank, Gaza, Israel, Jordan, Lebanon, Syria, North America, and Europe. (Just under half of Palestinians worldwide live in Palestine or Israel; the other half are divided between refugees in the neighboring countries and refugees/immigrants in the wider Middle East and the rest of the world.) The core of the document makes its demands clear:

> We, representatives of Palestinian civil society, call upon international civil society organizations and people of conscience all over the world to impose broad boycotts and implement divestment initiatives against Israel similar to those applied to South Africa in the apartheid era. We

appeal to you to pressure your respective states to impose embargoes and sanctions against Israel. We also invite conscientious Israelis to support this Call, for the sake of justice and genuine peace.

These non-violent punitive measures should be maintained until Israel meets its obligation to recognize the Palestinian people's inalienable right to self-determination and fully complies with the precepts of international law by:

1. Ending its occupation and colonization of all Arab lands and dismantling the Wall;

2. Recognizing the fundamental rights of the Arab-Palestinian citizens of Israel to full equality; and

3. Respecting, protecting and promoting the rights of Palestinian refugees to return to their homes and properties as stipulated in UN resolution 194.[13]

One of the reasons that the BDS call is so important to Adalah-NY is that it emerged from the political preferences of a diverse group of Palestinians, representing both different political tendencies (Islamist, nationalist, and others) and different experiences of Palestinianness, including not only Palestinians in the West Bank and Gaza but also those inside Israel and those living outside historic Palestine. Failures to integrate the perspectives and opinions of all of these groups have been a major driver of intra-Palestinian political chaos and a factor in the weakness of progress in achieving the national movement's goals. The BDS call avoids this. One member said that the BDS manifesto was one of the most agreed-upon documents by Palestinian civil society, in the territories, among refugees, in Israel, and in diaspora, in ten years and then added parenthetically that maybe it was more than ten years because he's not sure that that many people agreed with the Oslo Accords, the agreement that led to the current form of Palestinian semiautonomy in the West Bank and Gaza. This comment led to a round of sarcastic snickers around the room, which implied that the group was familiar with the Oslo Accords as well as the strong opposition it received at the time from both left and right critics in Palestinian politics and the general consensus among most Palestinian political analysts today that it has been a disaster for Palestine and is unlikely to lead to a just resolution for Palestinians.

The BDS call is more than a founding document for Adalah-NY. Interaction with the international BDS movement and its leadership inside Israel and Palestine directly influences the organization's work. The selection of protest targets is justified through recourse to specific calls from PACBI, the Palestinian Campaign for the Academic and Cultural Boycott of Israel, and the Palestinian BDS National Committee, both of which are organized primarily from within Israel/Palestine. In addition, members of Adalah-NY reference concrete relationships with activists inside Palestine and use those connections to explain specific actions. For instance, Adalah-NY hosted a screening of *Bil'in Habibti/ Bil'in My Love*, a film made by an Israeli anarchist about the struggle against the Israeli Separation Wall in Bil'in.[14] The screening was held at the Salam Lutheran Arabic Church in Bay Ridge, making it the only event I was able to observe where Adalah-NY reached out to members of the new immigrant communities in the outer boroughs. The members introducing the film explicitly connected the struggle in Bil'in to their current campaign for the boycott of Israeli jeweler Lev Leviev, who had a store on Madison Avenue in Manhattan and owned rental properties in the city. They explained that Leviev was involved in the building of the settlements threatening Bil'in and was suggested as a boycott target by members of the Bil'in Popular Committee (the local organization featured in the film). Another speaker, a non–Arab American, talked about his specific moral duties as an American whose state supports Israel and that BDS is a tactic that Americans can use. When a question was asked about the Jewish community's opinion on BDS, the reply was that Jewish members of Adalah-NY work on these matters "within their own community." When an Arab immigrant man in the audience suggested that Palestinians should use force to return to their homes, the person leading the discussion quickly moved the conversation back to being about acting in solidarity with specific groups: "We're talking about this call and these nonviolent actions. Bil'in and Budrus, these two villages doing nonviolent actions, are getting their land back! These are the methods they want us to support. We can do this; we can call on our institutions to change. That's our purpose, what we can do here."

Within the organization, the dynamics of identity and solidarity were formulated differently. Members behaved as if their individual identities, as Jews or as Palestinians or Arabs, were primarily important for public-facing reasons. Many Jewish members felt singled out by reporters interested in BDS, as if their identity as Jews made their political position more legitimate. All members talked about trying to get the reporters to talk to the Palestinians, both Palestinian members of Adalah-NY and Palestinians within Israel/Palestine who were involved in the BDS movement. Jewish members of the group were also active members of specifically Jewish anti-Zionist, pro-Palestine, and anti-occupation activist groups and engaged in those groups on behalf of BDS as a strategy, and on following the Palestinian boycott call rather than generating separate boycott guideline.

As the story about Bil'in highlights, Adalah-NY's relationships to Palestinians in Israel/Palestine are with concrete individuals and organizations, rather than the vague statements that Al-Awda made. Several times during my fieldwork, Palestinian BDS activists were arrested and jailed in Israel. Whenever this occurred, the activist was referred to by name (frequently only first name) in conversation, and protests, press releases, and media bulletins propagated the activist's story. Leaders in the Palestinian BDS movement were regular correspondents with members of Adalah-NY, and emails were forwarded to the listserv from them. Generally, they were referred to by first names in conversation. Adalah-NY also made sure to keep PACBI informed about actions they do, and when a member of PACBI needed to be contacted, someone at the meeting would say "who's going to email [name]?" and another member would volunteer to do it.

The concrete nature of these connections is not merely an artifact of organizing; Adalah-NY members and the individuals they work with in PACBI and in Bil'in know each other personally and in at least one case are related. After the NYCBI-Adalah-NY merger meeting, two members, one Jewish, one Palestinian, were standing around talking about the Gaza Freedom March, from which the Jewish member had just returned. The just-returned member had gone on the march with the Palestinian member's cousin. The Palestinian member expressed concern about his legal status, participating in the demonstration, and the Jewish member reassured her that he had been safe, and then told a funny story about him mocking her singing in a video of one of Adalah-NY's actions. "Oh, sure," she said, rolling her eyes, "I'm worried about him, and he's making fun of my singing."

Figure 5.3. Members of Adalah-NY protest in front of the Leviev jewelry store on Madison Avenue in Manhattan, October 17, 2009. While Leviev's store was a frequent protest location, this particular protest concentrated on the arrest and detention of Mohammad Othman, an activist with Stop the Wall, a Palestinian group that organizes against the Israel-built separation wall that cuts off West Bank communities from each other and often from their agricultural land, while intending to serve as a security barrier for Israeli communities. Othman was detained in late September 2009 and released in January 2010. Many of Adalah-NY's members had met him, either in Palestine or when he traveled abroad. Three of the signs used at this protest (those about Bil'in and Jayyous and the one with the diamond drawn on it) were used repeatedly at different Adalah-NY protests; the one about Mohammad Othman was made specifically for this protest and used at Leviev protests until his release. Photo by Adalah-NY.

The Palestinians invoked in Adalah-NY's actions are always concrete individuals, part of specific movements. There is no generic "Palestinian people" who have unproblematic needs, desires, or political positions. The BDS document, for instance, is described as having wide support in Palestinian civil society, but isn't viewed as the universal word of "the Palestinian people." The discourse of solidarity that Adalah-NY uses in its work requires as its Other not a loosely defined Palestinian people but specific groups engaged in political mobilization on the ground. While Palestinians may differ from each other, these particular Palestinians have both legitimacy in their lived experience to motivate their activism (and Adalah-NY's activism on their behalf) and a program of action that appeals to Adalah-NY's members.

Although members had different identities—the group includes Palestinians, non-Palestinian Arabs, Jews, and some who were none of the above—within the group, there was not a sense that identity had to be actively managed to ensure justice between members. In fact, the common practice of balancing identities among members to ensure representation of all issues came in for affectionate teasing. At a meeting shortly after the NYCBI/Adalah-NY merger, someone was needed to head up the task of organizing the next meeting. A male NYCBI member volunteered, as did a woman who was involved with both organizations. "Now wait," she said, jokingly. "We need balance. We need a NYCBI person, an Adalah person, a woman, a man, a Palestinian, a Jew, a white person." "Hey, we've got all that," he said. "Though," gesturing to his hippie ponytail, "we do have the same length hair." "Too true," she said. While the group tried to prioritize getting Palestinian voices heard among outsiders, among members there was enough shared trust that there was no need to regulate or highlight members' identities.

Adalah-NY's emphatic use of solidarity frames, emphasis on Palestinian voices within the organization and in Palestine, and internal practices of diversity and equality form a conscious response to the problems of political engagement for Arab- or Palestinian-identified advocates for Palestine. Strategically, it uses its non-Arab members to support Palestinian voices and perspectives and keep them at the center of the conversation, while also ensuring that, internally, Palestinian identities are held as less fraught or anxiety-provoking than they might be in more mixed company. But articulating this does not require the sort of totalizing narrative of Palestinianness that Al-Awda uses to accomplish much the same task. The use of Jewish voices to authorize Palestinian voices also helps to remove some of the barriers to Palestinian access to practical discourses. Alone, this tactic is insufficient, but paired with others it helps to alter the conditions of political engagement.

"Fact-Based" Argumentation

One of the first descriptions of Adalah-NY's work that they put forth at their open meeting was "fact-based," with a strong grounding in research and the intention to gain concrete victories. While other Palestine activism groups issue statements, hold actions, or present lectures, Adalah-NY concentrates on limited, specific actions, which it backs up with intense research that other groups can use to carry out their own actions later.

For instance, my first task once I was attending meetings was to help prepare some research on the investments of TIAA-CREF, a large retirement fund serving academics and health care professionals. TIAA-CREF had originally been the target of a campaign to divest from Lev Leviev's company, Africa-Israel, but had sold their shares before the campaign went public, apparently for unrelated reasons. A group Adalah-NY often worked with, Jews Against the Occupation, was considering a larger campaign against TIAA-CREF to divest from all occupation-concerned businesses, and Adalah-NY had offered to do some preliminary research for the project.

Adalah-NY's members were confronted with a large pile of financial statements listing TIAA-CREF's stock holdings and had to determine how much TIAA-CREF had invested in Israeli and occupation-profiting businesses and in which ones. Members of the task force looking into the project first had to determine that none of the reports were duplicates, which required consulting people with expertise in nonprofit finance. We then had to comb through each individual report searching for companies of interest. I personally was assigned a three-hundred-page report and a list of twenty companies, and other members took similar tasks. Together, we compiled a large spreadsheet of TIAA-CREF's investments in boycottable businesses. At this point, the group collectively decided "not to put any real effort" into the issue but to be on call to run street demonstrations in support of a campaign launched by Jews Against the Occupation or other groups and to pass over our research to them. By the winter of 2011, Adalah-NY had taken up TIAA-CREF divestment as a major campaign and was holding protests at their New York headquarters.

This level of research was standard for all of Adalah-NY's campaigns. Their goal was to produce evidence, drawn from sources with high cred-

ibility, that they could use in campaigns to convince others to participate in a boycott. For instance, their research dossiers on Lev Leviev
included information about not just his work as a builder of settlements
but also questionable behavior by his security staff in Angola, his history of involvement in South Africa, and tenants' rights violations in
his apartment buildings in New York. With these different sorts of data,
they then publicly contacted charitable organizations (such as CARE
and UNICEF) that he supported and celebrities who wore his jewelry
and asked them to renounce him in an attempt to undermine the support for his business.

The focus on facts and evidence as a part of a protest and argumenta-
tive strategy was central to how Adalah-NY chose targets and actions.
One of their major goals as an organization was to have concrete successes. As one of the facilitators at the open meeting explained, they
thought it was morally incumbent that they actually achieve results because there are lots of Palestine actions that go on for years and years
and never accomplish anything. Therefore, they choose the targets of
their campaigns carefully. Of all the companies involved in the building
of settlements, Adalah-NY chose to focus on Lev Leviev as a boycott
target because his case had strategic advantages: he was building settlements in towns they had direct connections with, had New York offices
and properties, and was connected to other sorts of human rights violations in other contexts. During the NYCBI/Adalah-NY merger, the
various campaigns the two groups ran were ranked, and it was collectively decided to end a boycott campaign against Motorola (which sold
communications and security technology to the Israel Defense Forces)
because members found that it was difficult to frame and communicate the reasons to boycott Motorola and because they had yet to have
a visible success that could be used to promote the campaign and build
momentum. The Leviev campaign, however, was continued because it
had produced successes for years and there seemed to be some hope of
Leviev eventually going out of business.

In addition to the high level of research and documentation being
tied to Adalah-NY's desire to achieve concrete goals, it also underpinned
the organization's attempts to connect with the media. By marshaling
research and being able to present a wealth of data to journalists, they
were able to build what a member called "relations of trust" with jour-

nalists. This resulted in several of their campaigns getting local media coverage from television and print media, in addition to regular coverage in alternative and activist media (such as Indymedia and the Electronic Intifada). This is most definitely the exception in the field of Palestine activism and in general for activist groups that are not highly professionalized.

Just as Adalah-NY used the identities of participants as a way to maximize their access to a broader sphere of contestation, they also used research to bridge their way into the public sphere. If you want to ask UNICEF to stop accepting sponsorship from a business (which they did—Lev Leviev had been a donor, but was quietly dropped), you need to present information making your case in a clear way that emphasizes the most objective sources possible—financial disclosures, public reports, detailed reports from the ground. The more evidence (and the more nonparticipants are likely to assess it as valid), the more likely that mainstream discourses might admit that information into debate.

Performance as Communication

New York City's street life is cacophonous: there is always something or someone to look at, particularly in Manhattan. The normal practice among New Yorkers is to ignore most of the visual and auditory distractions around them, whether a celebrity on the street, the flashing lights of Times Square, the Showtime guys performing on your subway car, or a demonstration happening outside a store. Adalah-NY favors street protests as a tactic, but they carry them out in an environment where passersby always have something else to look at and are culturally trained to disengage with their surroundings, over and above the general unwillingness of Americans to engage in exchanges about Palestine.

Adalah-NY's answer is layered, site-specific performances that use multiple methods in order to communicate actively with both passersby and people elsewhere. Their actions are always closely tailored to a single theme, target, or area of discourse. Signage and chants are clear and directly relevant to the specific protest rather than being generic. For instance, Leviev protests focus on the problems with his actions, such as settlement building or particular injustices in villages affected by the settlements he funds. Other protests focus differently. Adalah-

Figure 5.4. A participant in the Adalah-NY/Jews Against the Occupation protest of the Hebron Fund dinner at Citi Field holds a sign. The protest was held outside of the headquarters of Major League Baseball in Midtown Manhattan (rather than at the stadium in Queens). The Mets logo stickers were purchased for this protest and distributed while signs were made. Meanwhile, members of Adalah-NY passed out fliers with details about the situation in Hebron and the illegality of settlements under international law. Photo by Adalah-NY.

NY members learned that a fund-raiser for settlements in Hebron, an incredibly fractious location in the West Bank that has in recent years seen a great deal of violence by settlers against Palestinians, would he held at Citi Field, home of the New York Mets. That protest included a variety of signs and chants about Hebron specifically and settlements in general. However, in an attempt to draw attention, they also developed a number of signs and chants using baseball terminology and metaphors, and drawing on the Mets' invocation of the integration of baseball via the Jackie Robinson Rotunda at the recently opened Citi Field. In both cases, the same people are protesting against support for settlements, but at Leviev's store on Madison Avenue they chant "From Madison to Palestine / Occupation is a crime," while outside the Major League Baseball (MLB) headquarters in Midtown, they chanted "Worse than trading Nolan Ryan / Palestinians are dying."

In addition to chants and signage, Adalah-NY produced protest-specific fliers to hand to those passing by, particularly those who might be shopping at a boycotted store. While the group has a number of generic fliers about BDS, such as one that lists ten key products to boycott, they ensured that the events and fliers matched in content. Outside Leviev's store, they distributed fliers about a political prisoner from the town threatened by Leviev-funded settlement building. Outside of the MLB headquarters, they distributed material about Hebron. The specificity of these materials, making concrete, specific claims, helps in preventing these demonstrations from becoming rote, part of the noise of city life.

Adalah-NY uses a variety of musical and dramatic performances in their work, with two goals. The first is to draw the attention of passersby, by being as dramatic a spectacle as possible. The second is to produce either photos or videos of these protests that can be circulated to people who were not physically present. So at one Leviev protest three young women in the group performed a version of the Beyoncé hit "Single Ladies," complete with the eye-catching dance, with the lyrics changed to be about the occupation: "It's apartheid so you shouldn't put a ring on it / Occupation is a crime so put an end to it." During the Motorola campaign, NYCBI and Adalah-NY members performed skits in Best Buy stores with a Spice Girls theme and intended them mainly for internet consumption. At a protest against the Israel Ballet performing in

Figure 5.5. Members of Adalah-NY and the student community at Brooklyn College protest against an appearance by the Israel Ballet at the Brooklyn Center for the Performing Arts, located at Brooklyn College. Several performed in tutus and masks, while others held signs with slogans such as "Don't Dance Around Apartheid, End It" and "No Tutu Is Big Enough to Cover Israeli War Crimes." Others passed out a mock program that included information about the company, edited to include material about Palestinian villages destroyed to make contemporary Israeli cities, and other political facts. Photo by Adalah-NY.

Brooklyn, they formed a large dabke circle outside the performance. At another protest against the Israel Ballet, they wore tutus.

These sorts of performances, which integrate as many of the meanings of the protest into an action that can be viewed at another point in time, are a hallmark of the form of small-scale creative protest actions that were pioneered by ACT UP in the 1980s and 1990s and spread more strongly through the anti-WTO actions in Seattle in 2002 and the protest movements against the US invasions of Iraq and Afghanistan. As Boyd says, movements in this tradition feel the need "to design [their] message strategically and consciously so that it hits home with the public in spite of how it might get distorted by the media."[15] Adalah-NY members are active participants in the post-Seattle wave of protest and activism that draws on this tradition and integrate its key practices about the role of creativity in gaining ground into their actions. These attempts to make direct contact with audiences and to make narrow, focused points of action also respond well to the problems of discursive misrecognition that Arabs/Palestinians and their political allies face.

However, this strategy has limits that its advocates rarely explore: that the eye-catching, dramatic, and circulatable performances may do little to actually make the case for the actions they support, at least not for those who aren't already mostly convinced. In the best case scenario, the performance creates attention, while the well-researched and specific advocacy materials do the work of encouraging viewers to take action, but this link is not always successful.

However, the creative and enthusiastic performances have an important function not detailed in Boyd's framing: they are fun. It is fun to sing with friends, fun to perform on the street, fun to cheer for your friends while they perform, fun to plan guerilla theater in a big-box store. Traditional demonstrations, with marching, speeches, and chants, can range from boring to frustrating and have a limited emotional range, centering on anger. But Adalah-NY's demonstrations are fun, and members enjoy engaging in them. (Personally, I had left activism for graduate school in part because I hated attending protests—but I found myself enjoying Adalah-NY's protests more than any I had ever participated in, and certainly more than Al-Awda's.) The performance and creativity in Adalah-NY's actions may do more to achieve and maintain group cohesion than ensure it gets its message out to the unconvinced. But that is necessary work for any activist group.

Conclusion

In some ways, the approaches toward performing and articulating identities that Al-Awda and Adalah-NY use in their work represent the spectrum between working to develop bonding and bridging social capital: either a set of strong relationships that bring similar people closer to each other or weaker relationships with a broader variety of people, including those different from one's self.[16] They also demonstrate the difference between Castells's notion of resistance and project identities: in the former, groups create communal heavens that allow them to practice their alternative form of identity in an enclosed, protected space, while in the latter, groups develop identities grounded in the need to live a world-changing project in public and try to convince others to join in and create the desired change.[17]

In general, they describe fundamentally different purposes that identities can serve for social movements. People's identities cause them to become interested (or uninterested) in joining social movements; people can also develop relevant identities through social movement participation, either assuming new identities (such as "environmentalist") or giving previously unpoliticized or depoliticized identities new political relevance (such as "parent" or "scientist," or ethnic, racial, sexual orientation, or other ascriptive identities). We can see both processes in Adalah-NY and Al-Awda's work: Palestinian and Arab (and in some cases Jewish) identities motivate people to become active in pro-Palestine activism, and participants develop identities as members of their groups, participants in particular broader movements, and actors for social justice.

But identities can also serve as a way of understanding a group's orientation toward nonparticipants. A group whose practices are inward-turning, self-reinforcing, meant to cement and strengthen a specific given community does so at the cost of strengthening and deepening its relationships and ability to communicate with those who do not share that identity, or those who do not share the particular political orientation of its members. However, what it gains is a protected space wherein those identities can be performed and reinforced in ways that prevent external interlocutors from shooting them down. Resistance identities become spaces where people can revel in their common identification with a particular way of life and practice of politics, and do so free of suppression. Although in some ways resistance identities seem depoliticizing, they are in fact a political response to the challenges of voice and action for those who have little space to be heard politically. Al-Awda's stated positions are not terribly concrete, and have little chance of being heard and accepted into a broader political discourse. (I highly doubt any of the observers of their rallies walked away convinced to change their mind on Palestine.) But they provide a means of access to a form of political action—largely for people who lack that access, for reasons of language, citizenship, cultural difference, or political position.

Adalah-NY, on the other hand, works from an identity framework that is designed to make it possible to connect to others. This means that less time is spent in the organization dwelling on or reinforcing members' own identities as Palestinians, as Jews, or as other Americans—and no work is dedicated to creating an idea of the organization as a coalition of identities or promoting the idea of working in collaboration across identities. (Remember the laughter at the idea that the next meeting's leadership should be "balanced.") Instead, it promotes the idea that people's identities matter because they are essential to understanding people's political experiences and perspectives—that Palestinians' direct experience of the occupation, for instance, gives them a perspective on it that must be accorded the first priority. It also emphasizes ways that people can use their common identities to connect in order to reach out to those who don't yet agree with them and try to convince them. But while this strategy might be better at connecting and convincing interlocutors, it is in no way guaranteed to do so. Adalah-NY identifies a variety of successes in their campaigns, and in general advocates of BDS believe that their actions are seen as influential. In fact, both the recent Israeli travel ban prohibiting advocates of BDS from crossing Israeli borders (including entering the West Bank and Gaza, which requires permission from Israeli border control) and the recent attempts at legislation to rule advocacy for BDS as hate speech are seen as signs that the strategy is working.

But the extent to which these conversations have gotten out into the mainstream is limited. The Park Slope Food Co-op (a bastion of left-wing lifestyle politics in Brooklyn) may have held a heated debate about whether to boycott Israeli products, but in the end it voted not to do so—and neither Whole Foods nor Key Foods, spanning the upmarket to down-market range of grocery stores in the city, have had any conversations about doing likewise.[18] Adalah-NY has not fundamentally changed the conversation on how to support justice for Palestinians, but it and other organizations making similar demands have started to be included in the conversation—incremental change that might be all we could expect on this issue.

The Israeli occupation of Palestine and Israel's ongoing conflicts with its neighbors were for years the most reliable issues on which Arab community activists could mobilize community action. When I was conducting the first phase of this research as a graduate student, it was the only transnational political issue around which Arab Americans in

New York were politically engaged; there was little to no organized Arab presence, for instance, in mobilization against the war on terror or US involvement in Iraq, at least not between 2008 and 2010. However, the dynamics changed in December 2010, when the wave of protests that came to be known as the Arab Spring or Arab Uprisings swept through the Middle East and North Africa. As politics in the region shifted, so too did political engagement in Arab New York.

6

Thawra fii Times Square

Revolution in Diaspora

When I began the research that became this book, I had described one of the areas of discourse I wanted to study as "Middle Eastern politics and US foreign policy." After all, I thought, there was a whole plethora of issues related to those topics that Arab Americans would have good reason to care about: US support for the Israeli government and military, the plight of Palestinians, authoritarian governments and US support for them in the interest of "stability," the ongoing occupation and reconstruction of Iraq, how the newly elected Barack Obama was going to shift policy toward the region. It seemed obvious that I would find people who mobilized around all these issues and I could learn what sort of politics they are engaged in.

I was wrong. While, yes, all of those issues are ones that Arab Americans have good reason to care about, and individual, politically minded Arabs in New York did think, talk, and write about them, there was no sustained, collective engagement around the majority of these issues during the time of my research. There was no Arab community in practice that was organized around these issues or took them up as a primary or even important issue. The only topic in this framework that could actually attract Arab New Yorkers in large numbers was support for Palestine, as described in the previous chapter. Time was probably a factor here. Had I been conducting my research at the height of the renewed antiwar movement and mobilization against the invasion of Iraq between 2002 and 2004, I might have been much more likely to find Arab people and groups engaged in that mobilization. But by 2008 to 2010, it no longer existed in a way I could track.

And as time and the universe would have it, politics began to change again as I drew away from the field. By December 2010 and January 2011, when a wave of attempted and successful transitions and revolutions began to sweep the Arab world, I was finished with fieldwork, focused on writing up my findings and preparing to move away from New York City for the first time in eight years, in order to submit to the whims of the academic job market. I watched as things changed in those faraway places I and my Arab friends cared so much about, and as Arab communities close to home began to talk about what was happening there, I watched out of the corner of my eye rather than being immersed in the politics as it happened.

While I was busy elsewhere, Arab New York changed in the wake of the Arab Spring, not radically, and not entirely. The changes that I document in this chapter grew organically out of the preexisting networks of community service organizations and Palestine activism that had predated the changes. But as politics in the Arab world changed, so too did everyday politics in Arab New York. This time saw the emergence of a new emphasis on national origin identities, as opposed to broad pan-Arab identities, as focal points for political and social engagement. Much like the massive political mobilizations back in the Middle East that inspired these changes, the long-term effects of these shifts are likely to be smaller than we might expect or hope. But they demonstrate that the ways identities and ideas about politics are articulated within Arab New York are not at all static and respond to shifts in the broader political landscape.

In this chapter, I explore how Egyptian and Yemeni communities and identities became newly relevant to community action in the aftermath of the Egyptian and Yemeni revolutions. Many Arab countries underwent relatively significant upheaval and substantial change or attempts at change during the Arab Spring period, including Tunisia's successful deposition of Zine El Abidine Ben Ali in January 2011, Egypt's successful ejection of Hosni Mubarak and his National Democratic Party in February 2011, Yemen's negotiated removal of Ali Abdullah Saleh in November 2011, Libya's brief and internationally supported civil war turned regime change through most of 2011 (to be followed by a second civil war in 2014), Syria's uprising in 2011 turning into a civil war that continues as of this writing, and Bahrain's protests for expanded democratic and human rights starting in February 2011 and continuing into 2012. However, activism in New York largely was limited to support for the Yemeni and Egyptian revolutions, likely because those are some of the largest national origin communities, particularly immigrant communities, in the city. (There was some activism among Syrians in support of the uprising, but it did not coalesce in the same way as Yemeni and Egyptian activism, and the long stretch of the war and attendant refugee crisis have resulted in an emphasis on humanitarian demands among Arab American activists rather than demands for political change.)

Both Yemeni and Egyptian groups' responses to demands for change in their homelands show similar structures. On the one hand, groups supporting revolutionary change were formed and held protests and educational events that brought together people under specific, national identity labels, aiming to both support the transitions and make demands specific to the American diaspora context. At the same time, new service organizations emerged as well under specific national origin umbrellas, changing the landscape of community organizing for people of all Arab backgrounds. This demonstrates, in part, the dialectic between registers of politics: moments of heightened political attention to communities spur the creation of social movement organizations to articulate new claims, which then help create conceptual spaces where new civic organizing can happen, which comes back to have effects for people's political development and understanding.

Two new elements of political discourse seem apparent from this period. The first is that Arab identity, as it had been utilized among Arabs in New York City, revealed its fractures under the pressure of a politics that pulled Arabs in many directions. Individuals may have related differently to their national origin identities at moments of crisis, and the blad that united the practitioners of 'arabiya (see chapter 3) may have suddenly proved to be not so shareable. Second, political actions taken under these new banners have been framed and presented in ways that conform to American political scripts, emphasizing questions of democracy and justice in ways that make their claims more legible to non-Arab interlocutors. These new discursive resources position post–Arab Uprisings Arab political speakers very differently toward non-Arab interlocutors, in ways that may (or may not) be sustainable over time.

The organizations I write about in this chapter either are defunct or have mutated from their form during this period (unlike the three major organizations I worked with, which are all still going strong). It would be easy to treat this period in time as a blip, not a sign of anything substantial in Arab political life in New York. But as ephemeral as the actions described herein were, their existence tells us something about underlying conflicts and needs within Arab American political life.

These groups also tell us about the problems of political organizing while Arab. In many ways, organizing in support of the Arab Uprisings is an unsurprising kind of political engagement for members of an immigrant community. Nearly every immigrant ethnic group has at one point had members using their position in the diaspora to support a particular political outcome back home. But the work of organizing along these lines is additionally complicated for Arab Americans, who bear the burden of being structurally prevented from full discursive engagement in American politics. Arab Americans had no preexisting political base from which to organize for their perspectives being heard on the transitions in their countries of origin. And both the Egyptian and Yemeni communities in New York are, on average, part of lower income brackets and speak less English—additional barriers to political participation and voice. The strategies that the groups use reflect their attempts to work around these barriers.

Ethnography at a Distance: A Note on Methods

This chapter demonstrates what Schatz means when he writes about the "ethnographic sensibility" as an alternate rubric for using ethnography as a method. Ethnography is about immersion, but immersion is not the point of ethnography but a methodological means to an analytic end. The goal is to be able to analyze what happens in a particular social space with respect to the identities, meanings, and values held by the people who participate in it, and immersion is the tool that allows the researcher to come to understand those identities, meanings, and values and apply them to the practices, actions, and interactions that happen in this space. Just as, on one side, ethnography and participant observation are cousin approaches, so are ethnography and discourse analysis on the other side, in that both seek to understand the contexts and meanings at work to a space/text and use them to open up analytic space around it.

I was not physically immersed in the Arab communities of New York during the period described in this chapter, nor as I was collecting data and writing it. But I bring the ethnographic sensibility to my readings of the data within this chapter. The questions I ask of my data (which largely consist of news and social media accounts of political actions and the functioning of organizations) are the same I would ask of an interaction I witnessed or participated in. What does this word or action mean? What can I know of these people by the signs they display? How does this connect to other practices? How does their interlocutor determine their choices? To answer these questions, I bring the knowledge I gathered conducting immersive ethnography to these new data and interpret them in this light.

Throughout this book, I have used social media data alongside data collected through in-person fieldwork. In this chapter, however, I rely on the data much more heavily, including Twitter posts and Facebook pages of individuals and organizations, along with videos and photographs of demonstrations posted by citizen journalists and activists. I believe that the digital lives of communities are deeply connected to their offline lives and practices, in addition to the norms and customs of the online spaces they are participating in. That is to say, there is a digital Arab New York that exists in tandem with the physical one—and in tandem with Arab diaspora and transnational Arab digital spaces and activist and political digital spaces and other digital New Yorks, all of which coexist with offline spaces of various types. The digital world is continuous with the physical, though it follows some of its own rules, just as behavior at home is different from behavior at the *jam'iyya* is different from behavior on the subway. Some of the data I collected digitally were a reflection of offline activity: records of political actions and meetings or announcements of events. Other data were more specifically digital. I use them together to reflect living communities and people, with lives lived both online and off.

New Mobilizations for Egypt and Yemen

Egyptian Americans mobilized nationwide in support of the Egyptian Revolution during January 2011, including holding demonstrations and parties in support of the transition in cities across the country. But what stands out is the centrality of two cities in that spread of protests: Los Angeles and its suburbs (especially Anaheim) and New York and its suburbs (particularly Jersey City). Protests in New York began on January

29, just four days after the January 25 protests that kicked off the eighteen days of the revolution. By February 5, there had been at least five of them. While some drew from existing political organizations—one of the largest protests was held with the support of Al-Awda and the International Action Center—the institution that emerged as the central actor in prorevolutionary organizing in New York was the Egyptian Association for Change USA (EAC). The EAC had its major chapter in Washington, DC, but was also hugely active in New York and New Jersey, holding regular protests and meetings. The organization described itself as "a group of Egyptians and Egyptian Americans committed to Egypt's democratic, political, social, and economic reforms."[1] It was closely connected to supporters of the National Association for Change in Egypt, the political bloc organized by Mohamed ElBaradei, but had no formal relationship to it, saying instead that they supported only the NAC's principles for change in Egypt.

The EAC was first referenced in the media as holding protests on January 29, both in Jersey City and in Manhattan, across from UN Headquarters. After Mubarak was removed from power by the Egyptian Army, it continued to carry out regular actions throughout 2011, in particular participating in the #Right2Vote campaign calling for Egyptians abroad to be able to vote in upcoming postrevolutionary elections.[2] They also organized protests to celebrate the first anniversary of the revolution, in New York and elsewhere. The New York group appeared to be dormant for a while after those protests; their website stopped updating, and their Facebook page shows no events until 2013. In July 2013, members of the EAC held a demonstration as a part of the Tamarrod wave of protests, which was supported by a coalition of actors who opposed the presidency of Mohamed Morsi, Egypt's newly elected, Muslim Brotherhood–supported president, and the Islamist-influenced new constitution promulgated under his watch. The Tamarrod protests helped bring about the military coup against Morsi, although some participants in the protest movement, including Mohammad ElBaradei, later opposed the return of military rule. The EAC strongly supported Morsi's removal, but has remained critical of the military government, and the elected, military-supported president, Abdel Fattah al-Sisi, who followed him.

Yemeni organizing in New York followed a similar path, with initial protests emerging from the community and then becoming institutionalized, although without the links to a formal political grouping in Yemen. The Yemeni-American Coalition for Change (YACC) was founded in 2011, in response to the growing strength of anti-regime activism in Yemen. They describe themselves as "an advocacy and solidarity group comprised of activists, professionals, students, teachers and concerned Yemeni-Americans, representing various Yemeni-American organizations, all uniting to support the peaceful revolution in Yemen and to see an end to violence against the protesters who demand freedom and an end to the vicious regime of Yemen's current president Ali Abdullah Saleh."[3] Most leaders of the group were highly educated Yemeni New Yorkers. For instance, Ibrahim Al Qatabi, one of the most frequent public representatives, works at the Center for Constitutional Rights, helping to organize the defense teams for Guantanamo detainees, and another member who was quoted in a *New York Times* article is a civil engineer who works for the City of New York. Another prominent voice was of Summer Nasser, who was a high school student in 2011, but spoke from the dais at multiple demonstrations. YACC managed to bring Tawakkol Karman to speak at their demonstrations in October 2011, just after she received the Nobel Peace Prize, and she spoke at other events by phone from Yemen.

The first protests that can be connected to the group were on September 20 and 24, 2011, which highlighted the deaths of protesters on September 18 in Sana'a and elsewhere in Yemen. Interestingly, some of these protests included cooperation with Syrians opposed to the Assad regime. However, the group's name does not appear until an October 28 rally at Dag Hammarskjold Plaza, across from United Nations headquarters. It seems likely that although the same people organized the demonstrations throughout, the actual organization arose between the protests. Their activities reached their peak in January and February 2012, when Saleh was in New York City receiving medical treatment. The YACC organized a total of four demonstrations against Saleh's trip to New York, using a wide variety of tactics such as rallies outside his hotel and at City Hall, and letters to Mayor Bloomberg, President Obama, and Secretary Clinton, as well as social media campaiging. They were able to receive a surprising amount of coverage in national and international news, as their protests were covered by the *New York Times* and *Wall Street Journal* and picked up by other papers as a result of a protester getting arrested after throwing his shoe at Saleh when he emerged from his hotel. However, events decreased in frequency after Saleh left New York. The last evidence I can find of the YACC carrying out an event was Ibrahim Al Qatabi appearing on a panel at Hunter College in September 2012 under his YACC affiliation.

Both the EAC and the YACC, as minor as their actions have been, represent something that was very new in New York's Arab organizational landscape. Though many Yemenis and Egyptians in New York had anti-regime political preferences prior to early 2011, and were highly critical of the governments they had left behind, there had never been sustained Egyptian or Yemeni organizing against those governments or to make demands on the US government to alter their policy toward them. But in the moment of crisis and transition that was created by the Arab Uprisings, Egyptians and Yemenis (along with Syrians, Tunisians, and Bahrainis) came together out of their preexisting social networks to attempt to join in the political work of revolution, even at a distance.

At the same time as these organizations were appearing and mobilizing Egyptians and Yemenis in support of revolutionary change back home, other organizations arose that used national origin identities to try to bring together Egyptians and Yemenis for community and social services, more along the model of immigrant-serving organizations like the Arab American Association.

The Egyptian-American Community Foundation was a preexisting organization that had focused on providing development support to Egypt. However, in the summer of 2011, it opened an office on Third Avenue in Bay Ridge (interestingly, not Astoria, which is more heavily Egyptian) to provide community services. The activities it attempted to provide duplicated, in many ways, services being offered by the AAA and the AAFSC; it advertised its ability to provide assistance with legal consultations, health insurance, and career advice, in addition to ESL and Arabic-language lessons. However, it also held monthly evening gatherings with presentations on subjects like business opportunities, public engagement, and drug awareness, as well as music performances and socializing. The EACF stopped holding these events or offering concrete services by 2012, although the organization still exists.

The Yemeni American Association of Bay Ridge (which later changed its name to the Yemeni American Association of New York, a name that had been used by an older but largely defunct organization in Gowanus, Brooklyn) also started in the wake of increased organizing in 2011. It is strongly linked to YACC, in that several of its board members were also involved in YACC and became more politically engaged through it. It aims to have a dual role, both to offer services and connections to Yemenis in New York and to inspire Yemeni support for development projects back in Yemen. Although it began operating in the immediate post–Arab Uprisings period, it is still much more embryonic—but unlike the EACF, it appears to be continuing to exist for at least the medium term, in part because of its committed and active board.

This blend between political organizing for change in the country of origin and organizing to work with members of the community here follows with some of the findings of previous research on transnational political engagement. Diasporas and immigrant communities have always retained ties to communities back home and often have taken part in freedom struggles, calls for political change, and development support to their places of origin, with these efforts emerging from diaspora or, in some cases, being solicited by states.[4] Research on Latin American immigrant communities in the United States has found that roughly a sixth of members of the communities studied regularly engaged in political action oriented toward their homelands,[5] and that ethnic organizations often blended approaches toward US-based issues and homeland politics.[6] That communities connected to the countries undergoing such major change would speak up and take action is unsurprising. But the consequences of this moment for Arab community politics in New York rely on how it reconfigures forms of identity and discursive framing, offering new possibilities for self-articulation.

From (Pan)ethnicity to National Origin

Nearly all forms of community or social organizing by people of Arab descent until 2011 had taken place either under the rubric of "Arab" or under religious banners, whether Muslim (which frequently involved cooperation among racially and ethnically diverse Muslims) or a specific Christian denomination (Coptic, Orthodox, etc.). Much organizing continues to take place under those banners. But the appearance of specific national origin organizations, both political and otherwise, raises the question of when and how individuals choose identities to use to build organizations and collective institutions.

Intersectional theories of identity propose that individuals experience their identities not in parallel to each other, but simultaneously, with layered, reflecting consequences for their life experiences. Most often, an intersectional approach is used to understand how different identities correlate to different political actions or behaviors—differentiating people along the lines of race and gender, for instance.[7] However, a key insight of Kimberlé Crenshaw's original articulation is her proposal that "the organized identity groups in which we find ourselves are in fact coalitions, or at least potential coalitions waiting to be formed."[8] That is, racial groups should be understood not as single, stable groups but as a coalition made up of men and women who share a racial identification. Such a coalition requires maintenance and political work to keep together.

I propose that Arab identity in the United States is best thought of as such a coalition—not just of women and men, immigrants and native-born, cisgender/heterosexual or LGBTQ-identified, Christians and Muslims, but of people with diverse national origin backgrounds. Rather than trying to sort out whether Arab American is a panethnic identifier (like Asian American) or an ethnic identifier (like Chinese American—another community with diversity to rival "Arab" for its breadth), I propose that instead we should think of it as an intersectional coalition. Any invocation of an Arab American community must be made of a coalition of people who understand themselves as Arab, while also understanding themselves as Egyptian, Yemeni, Syrian, Palestinian, Iraqi, and so on. In addition, they also understand themselves as having genders, religious identities, sexualities, class identities, and other relevant identities. But that organization of the community as a coalition is always contingent on the people who hold those different identities continuing to believe that their coalition is beneficial, that they are getting something out of it, and that there isn't a better alternative.

Why might the coalition have appeared so unified throughout the earlier phases of organizing in Arab communities in New York? I would argue that size is the major factor. While the number of people with Arab ancestry in New York may be larger than the number in, say, Detroit (77,515 people of Arab origin in Wayne County, which includes Detroit and Dearborn, and 81,827 in the five boroughs based on the 2009–2013 ACS tables), they make up a very small percentage of the population (less than 1 percent, in comparison to 4.3 percent of Wayne County). They are also an incredibly small community in comparison to many ethnic and panethnic groups in the city. After all, there are 2.3 million Latinos in New York, with more Puerto Ricans (761,655), Dominicans (607,736), Mexicans (308,952), Ecuadorians (184,905), and Colombians (98,294) than Arabs of all nationalities; there are also nearly 490,000 people of Chinese ancestry, and over 200,000 Indians or Jamaicans. By contrast, the only large ethnic communities in Wayne County other than Arabs are white, nonimmigrant ethnicities (especially Polish and German Americans), black Americans, and Latinos, especially Mexicans. Rather than a cacophony of ethnic groups taking up space, among which Arabs appear as a miniscule group among dozens larger or of similar size, Arabs in Detroit are a major demographic, larger than any other nonwhite, nonblack group.

Given the relative smallness of the Arab community in New York compared to its neighbors, it makes sense that, in the early phases of community mobilization, the broadest possible identity coalition would be used as a means of organizing, under either a religious banner or an ethnic one. After all, if individuals with different national origins know each other and share a goal of supporting community organizing, they would use the identity label that they share (Arab or Muslim) in order to label their organization. Groups like the Arab American Association of New York, Alwan for the Arts, and the Network of Arab-American Professionals used that rubric to bring together people who share an Arab identity, regardless of their other identities.

But organizations that come together around these identities can break down when they are no longer serving the purposes of all of their members—particularly when one group becomes dominant over others. This can happen with broad and common intersecting identities such as gender or class, or it can happen with more specific factors, such as national origin or political differences in the case of Arab Americans. For instance, the American-Arab Anti-Discrimination Committee has seen two prominent fractures in its attempt to use an Arab coalitional identity to maintain a national organization in recent years. In 2013, a number of women who had been active in the organization came forward publicly to state that multiple claims of sexual harassment had been made against the leader of the Michigan chapter, but that the national branch had not acted on them. A long debate about the validity of the claims ensued, and the leader was eventually removed from his position, but, among many feminist and progressive Arab Americans, the original unwillingness of the organization to take action was seen as exemplifying the problem of sexual harassment in Arab organizations as well as the unwillingness of those organizations to take a clear stance against it.[9] Two years earlier, the ADC had seen a controversy where a pro–Syrian Revolution musician, Malek Jandali, was uninvited from a performance at their national conference if he was going to sing his prorevolution song. Again, more progressive members of the community, particularly those who opposed the Syrian regime or supported transitions in other countries in the region, argued publicly about whether it was time to stop participating in ADC events or to start new organizations.[10] In the first case, gender caused a fracture, with a group of women and others who were concerned with sexual harassment choosing to disengage from the coalition identity in favor of supporting their own interests. In the second, the intersection of national identity and political orientation created a group that no longer saw itself as being represented fully or correctly by the coalition. In both cases, continued support for the organization that tried to be the political embodiment of the identity grouping broke down.

Although Arab identity as a coalition continues to function in New York City's community life, it is not immune to stresses and ruptures along the lines of national identity. In particular, Palestinians and their concerns have taken on a dominating role in guiding the coalition. Although Palestinians are not numerically dominant within the community, a number of key political leaders (including most of the founding members of the Arab American Association) are of Palestinian origin. In political organizing, only Palestine was a cause that could pull huge numbers of people to a protest or event. After all, freedom for Palestine (and opposition to Israel) is a central theme of regional politics for other Arab governments, one that translates well into diaspora organizing. Crisis is frequent enough to keep the issue feeling important and participants feeling engaged. If the conflict is framed as being important to all Arabs or all Muslims, then mobilizers can use these other identities in order to keep energy flowing toward the organization.

But this predominance of Palestinians and Palestinian identity in Arab spaces does not mean that non-Palestinians were entirely comfortable with it. At the bake sale where the members of Najmat Falasteen practiced, I was talking to one of the girls about the dance and she said, "Well, I'm Moroccan, we don't dabke," as a way of explaining that she was still learning. Yet dabke, a folk dance from the Levant, was presented within the organization as an "Arab" dance, in ways that Egyptian or other North African folk dances are not (such as at the bazaar, where the Egyptian folk dancers were presented as Egyptian, not universally Arab). Suleikha also, as she grew increasingly bitter about the AAA as an employee, would talk about identifying as Egyptian, *not* Arab. (Egyptian identity, with its ancient roots, location outside Ottoman Syria, and some of the least arbitrary national borders in Africa or West Asia, has some of the greatest potential for a strong identity as other than Arab, just as some Lebanese use Phoenician and Christian identities to do the same.) I argued in chapter 3 that, through interaction among Arabs of different national origins in diaspora, a notion of shared 'arabiya is developed, making it possible for different people to share an identity that can be the basis of community organizing. But the identities that are subsumed in this notion of 'arabiya are not erased in the process; 'arabiya as a discourse provides some opportunities, but does not totally replace its predecessors.

The Arab Uprisings provided a juncture where these national origin identities could push back against the single narrative of Arabness and bring their issues to the forefront. Mobilizations were specifically undertaken in the name of specific national origin communities, even if the attendance was pan-Arab. For instance, videos posted of early Yemeni anti-Saleh demonstrations called them demonstration of *abna' alyaman nuyurk* or *abna' jama'at yaman nuyurk*, sons of Yemen in New York or sons of the Yemeni community in New York. Similarly, a protester taking photos of participants at an anti-SCAF protest in Times Square labeled them *waladak ya masr* and *binatek ya masr* (your sons, oh Egypt and your daughters, oh Egypt).[11] Demonstrations were held not by generic Arab organizations but by Egyptian or Yemeni organizations. These are not generic "Arabs" or "Arab Americans," but specific communities with concrete ties back home.

At the same time, these events include other Arab-identified individuals, under a rubric of solidarity and pan-Arab support. The first demonstration against Saleh was held "in partnership with the Syrian community," and most of the September and October 2011 Yemeni protests included specific slogans against Bashar al-Assad as well as Ali Abdullah Saleh. For instance, protesters chanted *"la Ali wa la Bashar, wahed jahsh wa tani hmar"* (no to Ali and no to Bashar, one's a jackass and the other's a donkey) and alternated between calling Assad and Saleh dictators and chanting to get them "out the door." Another protest leader led the group in chanting "Free free Yemen, Free free Syria" and then went on to have them chant for Iran, Palestine, Egypt, Bahrain, and then added, "And you know what? Free free USA! We have many problems to resolve here." The EAC publicized demonstrations in support of Syria, Libya, Bahrain, and Yemen throughout 2011. One person interviewed at an EAC protest in May 2011 specifically identified herself as Lebanese in her explanation of why she came. And in September 2011, a "Freedom Square" protest was held by a number of groups, which specifically aimed to speak across the different uprisings taking place.

But within this explicit willingness to join Arab identities at these protests came a new desire to acknowledge differences. A woman giving a speech at the Yemen protest said during a speech about media attention, "To all my Arabs who were together in all the demonstrations, we were together in the winter, we were together for Egypt, for Tunisia, for Syria, and also for Libya, so please also be here for us, for Yemen." At the Freedom Square protest, there was a signpost with arrows pointing to Tahrir Square, Cairo (Egypt); Hama (a city in Syria); Tahrir Square, Sana'a (Yemen); Azadi Square (Iran); Avenue Habib Bourguiba (Tunisia); Martyrs' Square (Libya most likely, although there is also a prominent Martyrs' Square in Beirut); and Gaza (Palestine). A meme was posted on Facebook saying that "I was born in Tunisia, lived in Egypt, went to Yemen and Bahrain, and today I am fighting in Libya. I will grow in the Middle East until I make my way to Palestine. My name is FREEDOM!" Another one jokingly pointed out to Arab dictators that there were twenty-two countries in the Arab world and only fifty-two weeks in the year, meaning each revolution had only about two and a half weeks to fight if they were going to replace them all in a year, so please keep to the pace.

Statements like this demonstrate that Arabs (in diaspora and back in the Middle East) believed that they shared a linked fate across national identities and could all come together and mobilize together. Just as with the list of cities in the Freedom Square protest, these actions bring together all of the countries of the region but demonstrate that each country's experience of this moment of political upheaval would be different and that there were meaningful and important differences among different Arabs.

A survey of the long history of diaspora political organizing helps drive home the general point that political action increases based on the intensity of political upheaval or struggle in the country of origin.[12] What made 2011 a particularly interesting period for Arab Americans and diaspora organizing was that national origin interests and identities began to take priority over Arabness, or at least shared the stage. Most of the research on diaspora political engagement back home has been oriented around individual national groups, whether tied to an existing state (like the Chinese or Mexican diaspora) or stateless nations (like Kurds or Palestinians). But research that relies on diaspora communities as relating primarily to unified nations is hard-pressed to account for the status of a group like Arab Americans, who identify with each other across state borders but also differ from each other in ways that can cause conflict. For instance, Yossi Shain conflates Arab Americans' increasing political organization in the 1990s with their increasing ability to advocate for Palestine, without acknowledging that non-Palestinian Arabs might be interested in advocating for their countries as well or that Arabs might come together to advocate for another country.[13] What the example of the Arab Spring shows is that the conditions exist for Arabs to organize in national origin groups but also to continue to use cross-Arab identifications as a means to greater political organizing. The coalitional Arab identity can stretch to allow the identities that form it to speak for themselves, with the strength of the broader community behind them.

From Palestine Activism to the Arab Uprisings

Al-Awda was a participant in pro-uprising action, particularly before alternative organizing structures existed. For instance, the January 29 protest outside the UN, reported in the media as being organized by

Figure 6.1. A protest organized by the Egyptian Association for Change on July 8, 2011, near the United Nations, in support of the right to vote for expatriate Egyptians. Egyptian flags were a major component of the performance of the event, but note the pro–Syrian Revolution T-shirt on the child at the far right. Photo by Egyptian Association for Change.

EAC, was reported in online activist spaces as being organized by Existence Is Resistance, a Palestine activist group that regularly was listed as a cosponsor on Al-Awda events, and photos from the event show signs made in the format that the International Action Center produced for Al-Awda events, with different slogans and different organizational affiliations: an IAC sign saying "No More US $ for the Bloody Mubarak Dictatorship," an Al-Awda sign saying "Long Live the Egyptian Intifada," and EAC signs reading "Egyptian Blood Is Our Blood" and "Egypt's Struggle Is Our Struggle." In addition, an Al-Awda organizer spoke at the rally. The crowd at the rally visually resembled the crowd at an Al-Awda rally more than the crowd at, say, Adalah-NY demonstrations or even the participants at the Jersey City protest the same day or other EAC demonstrations later in 2011: the crowd was very gender mixed, with many of the women wearing hijab, and very large, the size of an average Al-Awda demonstration.

Al-Awda also participated in supporting pro-Yemeni-uprising protests. At a silent march down Atlantic Avenue (from a mosque down near the intersection with Flatbush up through the Arab strip) and then to Borough Hall, one of the featured speakers was a white man who was identified as an Al-Awda speaker. His speech, however, focused on the connections between the different Arab Uprisings at first and then moved to opposition to American military action across the world, Occupy Wall Street, and other left-wing causes. IAC also did not contribute signs to any of the Yemeni protests I was able to find images of. It may be that by the time Yemeni activists were organizing to support their uprising, the major attention of Al-Awda and other groups had turned to other issues.

There are other general ways in which both Yemeni and Egyptian protests in support of their respective uprisings more closely resemble Al-Awda demonstrations than those held by Adalah-NY. For instance, chants alternate between Arabic and English (with Arabic predominating), and the English spoken at the protests is largely Arabic accented. Looking at Yemenis and Egyptians, their communities are substantially less English-speaking than the general Arab population (11.2 percent of Yemenis and 25.5 percent of Egyptians speak English at home, whereas 31.7 percent of all Arabs in New York City do), which may influence why the demonstrations that arose at these moments were more bilingual and Arabic centered. In addition, the attenders at protests were more likely to have roots in outer-borough, recently immigrated communities in New York. Again, Egyptians and Yemenis are more heavily foreign-born than the general Arab population in New York, which may help tilt the balance. Although there certainly are Egyptians and Yemenis in New York who are more like Adalah-NY's members, they are fewer in number and the leadership of organized mobilization came from these outer borough working and middle classes, including professionals (such as Ibrahim Al Qatabi, mentioned above), with roots in these communities. Individuals with different class locations did support the same movements; Mona Eltahawy, a journalist who moves between New York and Cairo, was a featured speaker at an EAC event, for instance. But the core participants came from these outer borough communities.

American Registers for Arab Claims

While these protests demographically resembled Al-Awda's demonstrations and often seemed to have some collaboration with Al-Awda at their early stages, they were very different from Al-Awda protests in many of the claims made and arguments posed. These protests, perhaps unsurprisingly, borrowed substantially from transnational discourses, echoing the chants and styles of protests being carried out in Sana'a or Cairo, assisted by the physical movement of people from one location to the other and the digital movement of discourse, supported by Twitter, YouTube, and Facebook. At the same time, Egyptian and Yemeni organizers framed their claims and demands in ways that were compatible with preexisting American notions of the good in political life, particularly ideas about freedom and democracy. They also used national origin patriotism as a central part of their framing (in a way consistent with ethnic community pride) and made specific demands that did not fundamentally challenge the assumed norms of political life. This type of rhetorical argument reflects Shain's argument that "the aftermath of the cold war, when the principles of democracy and human rights reign supreme . . . should enable diasporas to become more effective in pushing policy makers to adhere to America's values of promoting democracy and an open society around the globe."[14] The problem with this for Arab Americans is that discursive misrecognition and ongoing political marginalization provide barriers to these gestures being useful. Arab Americans supporting transitions in their countries of origin could reach for and attempt to use these frameworks to position their activism, but they had no guarantee of success.

Freedom was a key rallying cry for all of the Arab Spring movements, and this was invoked constantly during protests supporting them. A young woman who had worked as a journalist in Sana'a spoke about the Yemeni people teaching her "the value of freedom," which she had never previously understood. Another protester yelled, "Raise your voice and call for freedom forever, now or never." Protesters also chanted *"hurri-yeh, hurriyeh"* (freedom, freedom) and were led from the dais in chanting "What do you want? Freedom! When do you want it? Now! *Al-sha'ab yurid isqat al-nizam"* (the people want the downfall of the regime). One protester held a sign which communicated a complicated argument about preferences:

All Yemenis want
*Freedom
*Civil Rights
*"No" to Communism
*Stop Killing People
It Is Enough!

Egyptians also used the idea of freedom as central to their explanations of their actions. A news story quoted one man as saying, "While it was 'extremely sad' to see the violence . . . 'freedom has a price,'" while another protester said, "It's a struggle for freedom, it's a struggle for values." A handmade sign held up at that protest read "Egyptians have earned their Freedom, Mubarak must go!" Many protesters invoked the notion of freedom together with the idea of rights: a chant at a #right2vote protest declared, "We are Egyptians / we have rights," and a speaker at the January 29 protest said told that crowd that "we want our free rights as anybody in the world, we don't need Mubarak no more." What the Egyptian people wanted and what the protesters supported them in demanding was freedom.

Freedom may be a generic rallying cry for political organizers in a wide variety of types of struggles, but in the United States it is strongly associated with American values. "They hate us for our freedoms," George W. Bush said, and many Americans agreed: *freedom* is one of those things that make America America. So this identification of freedom as the goal in Arab uprisings legitimizes those transitions in the eyes of American interlocutors. When Yemenis protesting against Saleh's stay in New York for medical treatment held up a sign reading "Land of Liberty Hosts Dictator," they repeated the notion that freedom should be identified with America—and that Saleh's presence on US soil violated that natural association. The speaker who asked participants to call for "freedom forever" followed that call by saying, "Raise your voice and don't be afraid. Here, you live in a country that is ruled by law, so take advantage and let your voice be heard." The sign quoted above demanded not only a generic freedom but also civil rights and denounced communism, in an even more American-friendly register. And the letter that YACC wrote to President Obama, asking him to stop Saleh's trip to New York, asked him to "adopt . . . a policy toward Yemen that

Figure 6.2. A poster for a demonstration against former president Ali Abdullah Saleh while he was staying at the Ritz-Carlton, organized by the Yemeni-American Coalition for Change. The Statue of Liberty dominates visually, with the much smaller image of a vampiric Saleh in the corner. Meanwhile, both the content and typeface of the text evoke the bloody repression for which protesters blame Saleh. Image from the Yemeni-American Coalition for Change.

honors the principles that Americans hold dear—principles of equality, justice, and freedom from tyranny." When Ibrahim Al Qatabi said in the *New York Times* that "Obama is still siding with dictators instead of those who stand for freedom," he presented it as an immanent critique: America should have nothing to do with dictators and everything to do with freedom. Freedom and America are repeatedly associated, which legitimates calls for freedom coming from the Arab world in the eyes of American interlocutors.

Closely bound up with freedom as a rhetorical element is democracy. Democracy and freedom are often presented as synonyms in American political discourse that define what it means to be American. And plenty of the claims made in Egyptian and Yemeni (and other) protests in New York joined these together. An Egyptian protester quoted in one news story said, "We want people who know democracy. We want somebody we voted for, we never vote for him. He just fake the election and they think this is freedom. This is not freedom," evoking Mubarak's history of vote fraud (and the fundamentally rigged nature of elections in a one-party state). The EAC shared an invite on Facebook for a protest called "Rally in Solidarity for Democracy in the Middle East," which specifically called for people to support "the brave protestors in Syria, Libya, Yemen, and Bahrain as they struggle for democracy and freedom in their respective countries."

Both Yemeni and Egyptian demonstrators evoked a demand for democracy as intrinsic to what they (and protesters back home) were demanding. A large sign carried at the march through Brooklyn for Yemen read first *irhal* (get out) in Arabic, and then "The People Want Democracy" in English. Saleh was repeatedly labeled a dictator, the exact opposite of a democratically elected leader. In the same letter to Obama quoted above, the YACC argued that "we believe that by denying President Saleh sanctuary in the United States, we can demonstrate to Yemenis in good faith that we affirm democratic principles in this country." Here again the association between the United States and democracy was reaffirmed.

Talk about revolutionary changes in Egypt also invoked the primacy of democracy. A sign posted outside the Islamic Center of Bay Ridge calling people to protest before Mubarak stepped down in Egypt read, "Come support democracy and human rights in Egypt," according to a reporter visiting the mosque.[15] More telling is the role that invocation of democracy played in the way Egyptian American support for the revolution was presented in the press. A piece in the *New York Post* said an Egyptian American activist "has spent years fighting to bring democracy to her native land."[16] A later *Post* piece on Marty Markowitz, Brooklyn Borough president, raising the Egyptian flag outside Borough Hall had Markowitz saying that he "stood in solidarity with Egypt's pro-democracy protestors," "drawing similarities between the Egyptian Revolution and the American War of Independence," and saying "the American Dream is now the Egyptian Dream."[17] The demands continued to be used even after Mubarak had fallen: a sign at a #right2vote protest read simply, "This is what democracy looks like."

These comparisons are unsubtle, lack any substantive engagement with what democracy means (for instance, they do not engage with the future probability of Islamist government), and compare apples to oranges in terms of democratic transition. But they are rhetorically powerful, connecting Arab protesters to American icons and ideals and making space for Egyptian or Yemeni Americans to be proper democratic subjects while still being substantive advocates for their countries.

In addition, the clearest and most specific demands put forward by the protesters are well in line with frames about democracy. The YACC was closely involved in calling for Saleh to be removed from the United States, which involved specific calls on the US government to do something within their power (to revoke his diplomatic immunity or not issue him a visa) and to match American values. EAC's call for Egyptians abroad to have the right to vote in Egyptian elections was also fundamentally about democratic values, even if the demand was focused abroad. (Egyptians in diaspora did gain the right to vote while abroad, but participation was high only in the Gulf states; only about 5 percent of Egyptian Americans who were eligible to vote did so.)

Throughout these protests, the status of the protesters as American, as well as Egyptian or Yemeni, was reaffirmed. Sometimes this was through the recourse to American legitimizing norms, such as democracy or freedom. In fact, one speaker at a Yemeni protest did it through recourse to the discourse of antiterrorism, calling Assad and Saleh "the biggest terrorism [*sic*] of humanity." But others did it through active invocations of their Americanness. The letter by the YACC began by saying, "We write as concerned American citizens," and framed their demand for Saleh's visa being revoked by saying, "As American citizens, we see no reason why a man with as much blood on his hands as President Ali Abdullah Saleh should continue to enjoy the protection and support of the United States." A protester against Saleh at the Ritz even was quoted as saying, "I pay 30% taxes, and my money goes to protecting a dictator?," invoking an incredibly American political voice, that of the taxpayer.

At the same time, they also spoke as patriotic Egyptians or Yemenis. There was no rejection of their national origin identities. Yemeni and Egyptian flags were as omnipresent at these protests as Palestinian flags are at Palestine protests. Yemeni protests even began with the playing of the Yemeni national anthem, and a protester at one of them began his talk by invoking, *"Balady yaman wa suriya al habibatain"* (my beloved countries Yemen and Syria). A sign at a #right2vote protest read, *"misr lilkul al-misriyeen, mughtirbeen wa fii al-miyadeen"* (Egypt for all Egyptians, abroad and in the squares), while others said, "Egypt for all Egyptians" in English or "We are Egyptians too." Participants in these movements admitted the hyphenated nature of their attachments and legitimated their political action with regard to both of their identities. They were proper Americans and proper Egyptians/Yemenis at the same time.

This conscious linkage to normative American frameworks and values can be understood as a response to the problems of finding a political voice as an Arab American. In some ways they constitute a parallel to forced speech situations, although much more voluntary: we will avow our commitment to your values before you can even question them. By emphasizing the congruence between their goals and fundamental American values, political actors try to limit the space possible for interlocutors to move them from a category of person who can be heard to the category of person to be ignored. Look, they say, we sound like you, we believe what you do, we share your goals and ideals. Share this goal with us because we share these others with you. Listen to us because we are saying things you know how to hear.

But not every speaker can use these rhetorics in order to frame their words. No matter how much pro-Islamist Egyptians use the idea of democracy to talk about their opposition to the military deposing Morsi, their support for an Islamist still marks them outside the bounds of what can be heard in American political discourse. Palestinians advocating for a single state between the river and the sea likewise have almost no access to similar discourses. But in the moment of the start of the Arab Spring, when the transitions in the Arab world could be understood by Americans as democratic and freedom loving, these organizations were able to advance these positions to try to make space for themselves in public conversations.

Conclusion

The Arab Spring moment has passed; Egypt has seen four governments since Mubarak left power, Yemen has moved from one crisis to the next, Syria is torn apart through bloody civil war. The support for something new, something different in Arab organizing in New York that arose during the time of the Arab Uprisings, however, has not entirely disappeared. Just as the politics of the region is irreparably changed by the fact that, at one point in time, popular movements were able to fundamentally change how power was exercised, or at least who was exercising that power, the people who make up Arab New York now have new experiences that shape their identity—as Arabs, as people with particular national origin, regional, or religious identities, and as Americans. And how non–Arab Americans looked at their Arab interlocutors may have expanded as well. The framing and reception of pro–Arab Spring demonstrations help to show that there is a possibility for new political identities for Arabs in the United States to occupy: ones as democratic citizens, transnationally attached but discursively American. The Islamophobic and anti-Arab racist misrecognitions are still present, but the possibility for other ways to relate to each other was made visible. Change is never linear—the Arab Spring showed us that, as if we didn't already know—but it is change, and discourse is nothing if not changeable.

Conclusion

I am starting to write this conclusion on the rooftop terrace of a Mexican restaurant in Ramallah, the administrative center of the Palestinian Authority, drinking *limoon wa na'na'* and listening to the aid workers at the next table tell war stories. It was in this city, over a decade ago, that my interest in Arab Americans was born, as I met dozens of American Palestinians visiting their families during August vacation and started to wonder how their experience of politics was developed by being located in between these two specific places.

I wonder if it was here, and in my study of Palestinian politics in general, that I became convinced of the centrality of the everyday to politics. This is a place where the color of your license plate determines what roads you can drive on. Your choice of airport when arriving from abroad is a statement of your politics, or maybe just an effect of whether you've ever had a *hawiyya* (Palestinian ID card). The *sulta* (Palestinian Authority, the de facto government of Palestine) is running an ad on the electronic billboard outside my hotel room balcony, telling people not to buy settlement products (complete with a graphic of shaking hands crushing a peasant woman). I will be drastically overcharged for the terrible burrito I order tonight because Palestine lacks a national currency, and my card will accidentally be charged in dollars instead of shekels. All of this is politics, and all of this is experienced through the everyday: in our daily purchases, our decisions of how to get from place to place, the landscape around us. This is a place where you cannot convince yourself there is a hard-and-fast distinction between what's political and what's not.

That doesn't make Palestine unique. I return home to Canada, a country where I am an immigrant waiting to acquire permanent residency. My family's finances are dictated by the fact that my wife lacks a work permit, and she won't be granted one until my status changes. In the federal election that had just happened as I write the next version of this conclusion, a major campaign issue was the restoration of door-to-door mail delivery in urban areas, and there are persistent rumors that people voted for our prime minister only because he's hot. (I don't see the appeal personally, but I'm probably just too gay to get it.) My elder son, an infant carried around Brooklyn during the writing of this book, now knows all the words to "O Canada" and none of the words to "The Star-Spangled Banner," but he still says he's an American. My younger one was born here, and I joke that now my family is the perfect embodiment of the first, one-point-five, second generation model of immigrant acculturation. In Palestine, you have no choice but to see that the political is deeply embedded in the everyday, and that the everyday is deeply influential for the political. But once you've seen that at work, you start to understand that this is a general condition of political life, not a specific one.

The Everyday Is Essential for Politics—and Political Science

This book sketches a picture of Arab community life in New York City in the late 2000s, in the space where 9/11 was no longer an immediate crisis and the Arab Spring was about to bloom. As such, it adds to the other pictures we have of Arab American community life: marked by difference, inflected by politics, deeply embedded in American systems and structures while still retaining cultural and social distinctiveness. In particular, I hope that describing the texture of Arab community life in New York helps us understand the ways that local Arab communities in the United States differ from each other—that Detroit is not a perfect mirror of the rest of Arab America, and that our accounts of how Arab communities become integrated into American politics must take into account the diversity of Arabs nationwide.

But I also hope to contribute to the framing of this relationship between the political and the everyday in the study of politics more generally. To be frank, we, as political scientists, do not do enough to intentionally and rigorously study the everyday dimensions of politics, despite the fact that most people experience politics most often, most pressingly, and most intimately in our everyday lives. We need to make room in our discipline for detailed, ongoing engagement with people's everyday political lives because the more we understand political systems and the working of governance and power as removed from the lives of people, the less we understand about how those systems of power actually work.

My definition of "the political" is expansive and includes forms of contestation over power in many sorts of locations. But even if your understanding of politics is limited to interactions with states and formal institutions of power, we must use the everyday in order to understand and gather information about politics. Without paying attention to the everyday, we are missing out on much of what actually happens in people's political lives and on experiences and influences that have a significant impact on what happens in formal political spaces.

We experience politics, first and foremost, in our everyday lives. The vast majority of people are not directly involved in the workings of state power and formal politics, and even those who are directly involved experience politics as much outside that process as inside. As this book has shown, everyday experiences are deeply politically important for members of Arab communities in the United States. Arab community spaces are where people talk about and form opinions of political issues, such as corruption in their countries of origin, assessments of American democracy and bureaucracy, and what they need to feel safe and secure in their new homes. The women in my ESL class had little to no engagement with the formal state or in traditionally political activities. What they had experienced was the daily interactions with the state in the form of police, schools, and social benefits, mediated through their relationship with an Arab community in practice personified by the AAA, which helped them apply for those benefits, register for school, and report crimes to the police when necessary. This exposure and engagement in a civic institution was not a preparation for politics but itself constituted a form of political experience and a location for contestation.

Adalah-NY's cultivation of "relations of trust" with mainstream media sources is equally an "everyday" political practice. The practice of developing a relationship of trust requires the creation and nurturing of relationships that have a certain form and are maintained over time. The relations and practices that constitute this desired trustworthiness (research, citation, understanding the variable value of different sources) are routinized, taken-for-granted, everyday occurrences in the life of members of the organization. But this set of very ordinary practices has an effect on how Adalah-NY is taken seriously by media producers, which influences its ability to be heard by others and effect the changes it aims to make—a manifestly political process. At the same time, the quite everyday locating of Al-Awda within Arab community norms and practices shut off these routes to the mainstream, limiting their ability to be heard more widely and perhaps to reach their goals.

The political changes of the Arab Spring were also manifestly political, but they were experienced by Arab Americans as embedded in their everyday lives, rather than taking place outside of them. People threw parties in their neighborhoods and looked to others like them, rather than strangers, to talk about the changes and their consequences and meaning. While some engaged in social movement organizing—more formally political—others built community institutions or experienced changes in how they identified as Egyptian, Yemeni, Arab, or Muslim. The large political processes that shook the world were made personal and were interpreted and had effects in people's daily, nominally non-political lives.

In addition to people experiencing politics in the everyday, the everyday is also a sphere rife with contention, much of it manifestly political. Think of the young women dealing with community expectations and the expectations of non-Arab outsiders as they try to participate in the public sphere. They must continually struggle against interlocutors simultaneously beloved, despised, and disregarded in order to continue to make space for themselves, to manifest change, and to shape and change public life.[1]

The call of the Boycott, Divestment, and Sanctions movement is also explicitly a place of everyday contestation. Activists ask that individuals alter their most daily practices (switching from purchasing Sabra hummus, owned by an Israeli conglomerate, to making one's own or buying a local or Arab-owned brand) and make choices in their recreational and social lives (not attending a performance by the Israel Ballet) to serve a political goal. The contestation around often this takes place in people's ongoing interactions with each other, as when Adalah-NY members hand out flyers on the street with a list of products to boycott or talk to people they know (virtually or face-to-face) in order to convince them to change their minds. Despite the profound ordinariness of the actions most people take in response to the BDS call, the Israeli government has taken action against it, including both public relations work to counter it and banning advocates of BDS from entering Israel (or crossing Israeli border security into the West Bank). In addition, pro-Israel political actors in the United States and Canada have gone so far as to propose legislation banning advocacy for BDS, including in New York State. Just because a political action is located in the everyday sphere doesn't mean its consequences are trivial. The very dailyness of these actions multiplies their impact and puts them front and center in people's political consciousnesses.

When people organize to make demands against formal political institutions, they do so from within their everyday spaces, identities, and practices. As different as Al-Awda and Adalah-NY's styles of political organizing are, both of them draw heavily from personal, everyday connections. Al-Awda draws groups of families and friends, people who already know each other, to come and attend demonstrations, swelling their numbers and reinforcing connections within the immigrant communities of New York and New Jersey. They also recruit new members out of personal interactions with folks who might already be primed to be engaged: recall the young woman organizer at the City College Palestine event, working the room to recruit new members—and the young woman who asked me, before I started graduate school, if I wanted to join Al-Awda because we were in the same community Arabic class. This holds for Adalah-NY too; its members are friends and relatives with activists all over the world, particularly in BDS movements and in Jewish pro-Palestinian organizations. Their personal networks strengthen their ability to mobilize, their information about action opportunities, strategies, and successes, and their commitment to the cause.

The sense of camaraderie and friendship among members within organizations and between different organizations is critical to their ability to function. Adalah-NY worked as well as it did and managed potential conflicts over people's identities successfully because the members were friends, or at least friendly. The Al-Awda organizer I interviewed told the story of the organization discovering two of its board members were undercover NYPD officers, during the broader citywide reveal of the NYPD's surveillance of Arab and Muslim communities. The revelation shook the organization, which understood itself both as ideologi-cally diverse (within a left/socialist frame) and representative because of the presumption of trust among board members. Violations of this norm do substantial damage to movements and are also deeply pain-ful to people working in them—a profoundly political sort of personal disappointment.

If we ignore the everyday, we miss all of this: the subtleties of con-tention, the processes by which movements and organizations form and stay alive, the ways successes are achieved. Much good research does end up noticing these sorts of factors eventually because they are inescapable—the role of personal relationships in mobilization, the in-fluence of identity on political action, how people learn about when to participate and how to think about issues from others. But we study these things out of the corners of our eyes, asking people about their social networks and who they talk with about politics on quantitative surveys rather than sitting down and watching people's everyday inter-actions. We turn the everyday into one variable among many and reduce it to something quantifiable rather than starting by asking what is hap-pening and watching to see what's connected and what its consequences are. In this book, I started by looking at the everyday, asking first what mattered to people's lives and then tracing the connections to politics as they inevitably became apparent. The result is a book that shows how everyday spaces and practices are deeply political in their own practice, not merely as shaping grounds for future participation—and that our understanding of politics, particularly in Arab American communities, is inescapably too thin if we ignore this.

Arab America in the Era of Trump

The original idea for the research that makes up this book was hatched in the late years of the George W. Bush administration, as I thought about the forms of hyper-surveillance, securitization, and political oth-ering that Arab Americans were subject to during the post–September 11 period. The data contained in it were collected during the Obama administration, a period when Arab Americans felt slightly more secure (if still under surveillance) but no more included in the American polity and when the collective anxiety of the early 2000s was wearing off. But I am finishing this book during the Trump administration, when a presidential candidate could run on open Islamophobia, xenophobia, and aggression toward the Middle East and then carry a general election. How different is it for Arab American communities under these three different periods? To what extent can my data, gathered at the center of this arc, help us make sense of the current moment?

As I am writing, the Trump administration is only eighteen months old, so it is impossible to say what may come in terms of government-led suppression or silencing through the rest of his term in office. Rather than try to predict, however, I want to point to what I see as a significant and meaningful change for Arab Americans at this particular moment, which is the gradual broadening of the political actors willing to invite them into dialogue, acknowledge their claims, and understand them as a part of American communities that should be a part of practical discourses. This is not to say that there is not still deep anti-Arab and anti-Muslim prejudice in the United States or that Arab Americans now have no barriers to accessing American political life. But there are more political movements and actors who are willing to treat Arab Americans as coparticipants in politics.

During the two years of the 2016 presidential campaign, most attention was paid to the frequency of Islamophobia among the Republican candidates, with Donald Trump as the clear leader but other candidates, such as Ben Carson and Ted Cruz, engaging in similar rhetoric. But while increasingly horrible things were being said on the right, all three major Democratic candidates made explicit statements that recognized Arab, Muslim, and immigrant Americans as members of the broader community of Americans. Bernie Sanders ran Arabic-language ads in the Detroit metro area, made campaign visits to mosques, and repeatedly condemned anti-Muslim speech. Martin O'Malley also visited mosques and drew parallels between prior discrimination against Irish Catholics and contemporary discrimination against Arabs and Muslims. While Hillary Clinton did engage in the predictable securitization of Muslim communities, highlighting their importance to fighting terrorism, she also repeatedly voiced support for Muslims as proper Americans and opposition to Trump's most ludicrous positions and put the parents of Captain Humayun Khan, a Pakistani American Muslim soldier killed in the war in Iraq, on the stage at the Democratic National Convention. While the Republican candidates were tripping over themselves to demonstrate their Islamophobia, xenophobia, and generalized racism in an effort to grab back votes from Trump, the Democrats demonstrated that Arab and Muslim Americans would, at minimum, be recognized as American citizens.

Democratic voters agree with the signals being sent from the top of their party. The Arab American Institute and Zogby released a poll in the summer of 2017 that demonstrated a sharp divide between Republicans and Democrats nationwide in terms of opinion of Muslim and Arab Americans.[2] A majority of Democrats had a favorable opinion of Arab Americans (58 percent, opposed to only 23 percent with an unfavorable opinion) and Muslim Americans (61 percent, while 15 percent had an unfavorable opinion); to put these numbers in context, a 2009 Pew Global Trends poll found that 86 percent of Americans of all races and party affiliations had a favorable opinion of black Americans. In the aftermath of the 2016 presidential election, Democrats also disagreed with multiple anti-Arab positions from the Trump administration and Republican party; they opposed a travel ban on Arabs (53 percent) and Muslims (59 percent), supported resettling Syrian refugees (60 percent), and opposed law enforcement profiling of Muslims or Arabs (53 percent). Republicans felt the contrary on every question; independents more closely resembled Democrats, but with less intensity. Clinton voters had stronger approval and support for Arab communities on all questions than did Trump voters. In the aftermath of the 2016 election, America was divided politically on whether Arab and Muslims Americans are worthy of being considered members of our political community, but a substantial proportion of the population, affiliated with a major party, seemed to be comfortable articulating positions that were more positive towards their Arab and Muslim neighbors.

Arab Americans are paying attention to these sorts of signals. Another poll by AAI/Zogby during the 2016 election cycle showed 52 percent of Arab Americans identified as Democrats, 22 percent as independents, and 26 percent as Republicans.[3] This was down from 2000, when 38 percent of Arab Americans identified as Republicans, 40 percent identified as Democrats, and about half of Arab voters turned out for George W. Bush. This shift toward the Democratic Party persisted even though Arab Americans were not enthusiastic about Democratic policy performance on issues they cared about. A plurality of surveyed voters rated President Obama's foreign policy performance as "poor" (31 percent of all respondents, including 14 percent of Democrats and 29 percent of Independents) and felt only "somewhat positive" about his policies toward the Arab world (40 percent of all respondents, including 45 percent of Democrats and 47 percent of independents). But 52 percent believed that Hillary Clinton would be better for relations with the Arab world ("Neither" beat Donald Trump, at 24 percent to 23 percent) and 70 percent stated agreement with a pathway to legal status for undocumented immigrants, a left–Democratic policy position. Although there is plenty to critique in the Democratic Party's outreach toward Arab Americans and the fit between Arab American policy priorities and conventional American parties, Arab American voters have reason to believe that there might be a chance with the Democratic Party to get at least some of their priorities heard.

One of the Trump administration's first actions was to use an executive order to ban travel to the United States for citizens of seven Muslim-majority countries, including the major Arab sending countries of Syria, Iraq, and Yemen. The first attempt at the order was a disaster—a poorly implemented policy that held up travelers with valid visas at US airports, trapped green card holders abroad, and caused chaos at major airports across the country. (Subsequent versions avoided some of the obvious pitfalls—permitting green card holders to enter, removing Iraq from the list because many Iraqi immigrants have served with the US military, and not trapping people in airports. After a wide variety of legal challenges, the Supreme Court finally upheld the a version of the policy in June of 2018.). What is particularly intriguing about the reaction to the ban is the speed with which non-Arabs and non–Muslim Americans mobilized to oppose it. Protests were held outside airports, shutting some of them down. While Muslim and Arab Americans participated in these demonstrations, they were not alone and were joined by hundreds of fellow protesters. The messages of the protests at the airports were that Muslim immigrants, particularly refugees, should be welcomed in America and are a part of American life. The lawyers inside the airports working to get individual travelers admitted to the United States came from civil liberties organizations, left-wing lawyers' groups, and private practice, and the majority were not Arab or Muslim.

The news media ran dozens of sympathetic stories about immigrants from the banned countries and families in the United States waiting to welcome members stuck abroad. In short, thousands of non-Arabs and non–Muslim Americans showed up to object to infringements on the rights of Arab and Muslim immigrants and refugees. This did not happen in the aftermath of the September 11 attacks. It did not happen during the rollout of the National Security Entrance-Exit Registration System, which required male immigrants from a list of Muslim countries who did not have citizenship or permanent residence to be registered and led to the deportation of hundreds of Arab Americans and the prosecution of zero terrorists. It didn't happen, even in New York, when the NYPD targeted Muslim communities for surveillance. It happened because Donald Trump signed a stupid, cruel executive order—but also because, slowly, in the fifteen years since the September 11 attacks, some non–Arab Americans have figured out that they have Arab American neighbors, have begun to take what happens to those neighbors seriously, and have been mobilized by the election of an open Islamophobe to take political action.

Finally—and most complexly—look at the new political career of Linda Sarsour. When I met her, Linda was "merely" the director of the Arab American Association and had just begun to interact more directly with local politics. After the revelation of NYPD spying, she became active in civil rights and anti-police brutality organizing in New York. This led to her being part of an Arab and Muslim solidarity visit to Ferguson, Missouri, after the death of black teenager Michael Brown at the hands of police and the military-level police response to protests after the officer was not indicted, at the beginning of what would become the Black Lives Matter movement. During the 2016 election cycle, she became a national spokesperson for the Bernie Sanders campaign, both helping with outreach to Arab and Muslim communities and representing them to white communities, eventually serving as a delegate to the Democratic National Convention. After President Trump's election, she became one of the national chairs of the Women's March on Washington. In the aftermath of the march, which was one of the largest political mobilizations in recent American history, she was in the media constantly, including being named one of *Time*'s one hundred most important people of 2017.

In many ways, Linda is a tokenistic figure for those who highlight her: a hijab-wearing feminist and mother of working-class origins but speaking the language of social justice movements. She's the one Muslim Arab feminist a lot of people know, which drives those who have been doing this work for decades absolutely up the wall. But now they all know one Muslim Arab feminist, which is one more than they knew before.[4] When Sarsour spoke in an interview about not believing that Zionists could be feminists (based on conceptualizing Zionist as an exclusionary, racist form of nationalism and feminism as requiring opposition to those exclusions), she was attacked by some but supported by others. This sparked a conversation, however flawed, about the relationship among Zionism, anti-Semitism, and feminism, in which Palestinian voices were included and not entirely silenced. Sarsour went on to give a commencement address to the City University of New York School of Public Health, despite protests against her appearance from those on the right.

Linda Sarsour has been given space to speak in public, appear as a representative of Arab Americans, and voice her positions complexly. She is challenged on them, but she is not silenced in the process. Debbie Almontaser, the proposed principal of a middle school that would emphasize Arabic and Middle Eastern studies, was not afforded that same space in 2007 when she defined intifada approvingly for a group of reporters. When Steven Salaita lost a tenured academic position because of his outspoken positions on Palestine in 2014, he was given space to articulate his political positions fully only in those communities most receptive to his arguments and remains without a permanent academic position, although he also has a substantial new audience. It might be the way that Linda frames her arguments or her value as a tokenistic figure or even her "right" set of connections to political elites, but she has been granted room by some majority American discursive spaces to articulate positions that deviate substantially from the American mainstream and to do it while identifying primarily as an Arab.

This is not utopia, or even minimal justice. The space for Arab Americans to identify as such and articulate diverse positions on political questions is small and fraught with possible failures. But there is some space where there wasn't before. And it appears where we might hope it to arise first: among left-leaning or even liberal multiculturalist social and political spaces. In *Uncultured Wars*, Salaita argues that the biggest failure to listen to Arab Americans comes from the left. Nobody really expects the American right to listen to ethnic minorities, religious minorities, or immigrants, but the left should listen and often pretends it does without letting anything sink in.[5] We are far from a perfect environment for those who have previously been ignored to have their positions heard and incorporated into practical discourses. But marginally, in small pieces, some room is being picked out. It is no longer expected by the near totality of actors in American politics that American Arabs and Muslims will be talked about without being participants. There are just enough people who understand that they need to be included as well. It is possible to recite something other than patriotic platitudes as an Arab American in public life, even if patriotic platitudes are what will be best received. This isn't justice, but it is *change*, which offers the potential for more change, regardless of how the president or other conservative power holders may act. The future is always uncertain, but the struggle for full political membership for Arab Americans holds the potential to yield results.

Conclusion

I want to end this book where I began: with the children whose faces I painted at that bazaar in August, in a park where Arabic music played over the sound system and hundreds of people came together to form a physical manifestation of Arab New York. They liked getting flags painted on their faces, but that wasn't all they wanted. They liked dancing to Arabic music, but that wasn't all they wanted to dance to. Moustafa Bayoumi's book about young Arabs in New York borrows W. E. B. Du Bois's line, "How does it feel to be a problem?" At that moment, those children weren't a problem. Their parents weren't a problem; even the government (represented as friendly census reps, city councilors, the DA's office) wasn't a problem. Their ability to exist as themselves in public found a space to be unconstrained, at least for a little while.

This is what conditions of justice for Arab Americans can look like: the ability to speak and act as oneself with minimal constraint. It shouldn't have to exist only within bounded community spaces. We need to find ways to manifest it within broader publics—even if it is challenging, even if it forces those of us in the majority to reevaluate our practices and thoughts. It does not mean abandoning practical discourse and reason giving in public: fundamentally, it means fixing them. It's a difficult task, but a necessary one, for those children with painted faces, for those teenagers painting them, for the parents looking on. For all of us, in the end.

ACKNOWLEDGMENTS

I would like to start by thanking the participants in the two key organizations who provided me access while I was doing fieldwork for this book. The staff, volunteers, and clients of the Arab American Association of New York and the members of Adalah-NY allowed me to participate in their work and lives and were willing to share their thoughts, process, and analysis throughout. In addition, I'd like to thank the members and leaders of Al-Awda NY whom I interacted with through this project, who aided substantially my analysis of intracommunity political dynamics and debates. Despite the tremendous diversity of opinions, preferences, and styles of action these different organizations represent, I came away from my fieldwork deeply convinced that organizing in Arab communities in New York is in the hands of impassioned people who are working for justice. I want to particularly thank the woman named in this book as Suleikha. She was a wonderful friend to me during my fieldwork, and I have enjoyed knowing her through the years since.

The New School for Social Research is a uniquely encouraging place to write a subfield-bending dissertation, and the support of my supervisor, Courtney Jung, my committee members, Tim Pachirat and Nancy Fraser, and my external examiner, Karam Dana, was crucial to the success of this project. So was the comradeship of many of my fellow students, in particular Jackie Vimo, Geeti Das, Natascha van der Zwan, and Josh Lerner. The financial support of an NSSR Prize Fellowship and Dissertation Fellowship also helped tremendously.

I also owe thanks to the faculty of Hobart and William Smith Colleges, which was an excellent place to teach and work. In particular, I'm thankful to the many friends whom I met through the new faculty program and with whom I shared a strong connection (and a lot of tacos), including Kendralin Freeman, Emily Fisher, Jessica Hayes-Conroy, and Robin Lewis. The members of the Department of Political Science, including but not only DeWayne Lucas and Stacey Philbrick-Yadav, were also excellent mentors through the post-PhD period.

I am extremely thankful to have ended up in the École d'études politiques at the University of Ottawa. Many thanks are owed to my school and faculty for being supportive of junior researchers, particularly in the provision of teaching support, course releases, and start-up funding, and to my colleagues for being inquisitive, funny, eclectic, and passionate. Beyond my school, I want to thank Nadia Abu-Zahra, my co-director in the Community Mobilization in Crisis project, whose generosity and collaborative spirit have led both of us forward in our work, and Françoise Moreau-Johnson, director of the Centre for Academic Leadership, who has provided essential support for my writing life since I arrived at uOttawa.

In addition to support from all of the academic institutions I have been affiliated with during this period (including the University of Toronto), I would like to recognize the material support provided by New York State's social welfare system, including Medicaid, Unemployment Insurance, and the Women, Infants, and Children food program. This assistance was crucial during both fieldwork and much of the writing of this book.

Many people have read and provided commentaries on chapters or the entirety of this book; their comments, suggestions, and ideas have improved it, though all remaining errors are my own. I thank Shabana Mir, Layla Goushey, Randa Kayyali, Patti Lenard, Diana El Richani, Emily Traynor-Mayrand, and Ainslie Pierrynowski for their thoughtful attention, as well as the three anonymous reviewers from NYU Press.

Finally, I'd like to thank my family: my nonbiological siblings, Isabel Youngberg and Jesús Chapa-Malacara; my mother, Rose Regan, and my late father, John Wills; my biological siblings, Debbie Powley and Tom Wills; my sons, Xander and Joshua Rapoport-Wills, and godson, Jason Boyer; and most of all my amazing wife, Kate Rapoport. The life of an early-career academic is hard; the life of her spouse is harder. Thank you for supporting me through four jobs, three weddings, two countries, and twenty years of life together.

NOTES

CHAPTER 1. EVERYDAY POLITICS IN ARAB NEW YORK

1 Ronald R. Stockton, "Arab-American Political Participation: Findings from the Detroit Arab American Study," in *American Arabs and Political Participation: Proceedings of a Conference Sponsored by the Division of United States Studies, Woodrow Wilson International Center for Scholars, May 5, 2006*, ed. Philippa Strum (Washington, DC: Woodrow Wilson International Center for Scholars, Division of United States Studies, 2006), 53–78.

2 Michael W. Suleiman, "A History of Arab-American Political Participation," in Strum, *American Arabs and Political Participation*, 3–26. At the time of writing it seems likely that Palestinian American Rashida Tlaib will become the first Arab Muslim in Congress, running unopposed as the Democratic candidate in the general election in Michigan's 13th electoral district.

3 Evelyn Shakir, *Bint Arab: Arab and Arab American Women in the United States* (Westport, CT: Praeger, 1997).

4 Dina Okamoto and G. Cristina Mora, "Panethnicity," *Annual Review of Sociology* 40 (2014): 219–239, 221.

5 "Arab community in practice" is meant to echo the concept of a community of practice, which appears both in the education literature and in the broader, practice-based turn in the social sciences, although it is not identical to it.

6 In situating my work in a framework of "everyday politics," I intend to gesture toward the scholarship that has shaped my interest in people's political lives in the broadest and least formally political sense: work like that of James C. Scott, who documents the dynamics of everyday resistance in agrarian communities, Lisa Wedeen, who explores discourse, resistance, and identifications in Syria and Yemen, and Katherine Cramer, who studies public opinion ethnographically.

7 Irene Bloemraad, *Becoming a Citizen: Incorporating Immigrants and Refugees in the United States and Canada* (Berkeley: University of California Press, 2006), 80.

8 Ibid., 199.

9 Sarah Sobieraj and Deborah White, "Could Civic Engagement Reproduce Political Inequality?," in *Acting Civically: From Urban Neighborhoods to Higher Education*, ed. Susan A. Ostrander and Kent E. Portney (Lebanon, NH: University Press of New England, 2007), 93.

10 Marianne Maeckelbergh, "Doing Is Believing: Prefiguration as Strategic Practice in the Alterglobalization Movement," *Social Movement Studies* 10, no. 1 (2011):

1–20, 3; Luke Yates, "Everyday Politics, Social Practices and Movement Networks: Daily Life in Barcelona's Social Centres," *British Journal of Sociology* 66, no. 2 (2015): 236–258.

11 Kimberly Creasap, "Social Movement Scenes: Place-Based Politics and Everyday Resistance," *Sociology Compass* 6, no. 2 (2012): 182–191, 185.

12 Todd Nicholas Fuist, "The Dramatization of Beliefs, Values, and Allegiances: Ideological Performances among Social Movement Groups and Religious Organizations," *Social Movement Studies* 13, no. 4 (2014): 427–442.

13 K. L. Broad, "Social Movement Selves," *Sociological Perspectives* 45, no. 3 (2002): 317–336.

14 Jürgen Habermas, *Moral Consciousness and Communicative Action* (Boston: MIT Press, 1990).

15 Michel Foucault, *The Archeology of Knowledge & the Discourse on Language* (New York: Pantheon, 1982).

16 For more on the spheres of recognition, see Axel Honneth, *The Struggle for Recognition* (Cambridge: Polity, 1995). For further elaboration of my analysis of his approach to recognition, as well as a broader development of the concept of discursive misrecognition, see Emily Regan Wills, "Polemics, Political Racism, and Misrecognition: Naming and Analyzing Prejudice Against Arab-Americans," *Constellations* 21, no. 1 (2014): 50–66.

17 Louise Cainkar, *Homeland Insecurity: The Arab American and Muslim American Experience after 9/11* (New York: Russell Sage Press, 2009).

18 To use the Habermasian language, their norms testing and their criticism of normative agreements that have apparent consensus are not accepted and their reasons and argumentation are denied legitimacy.

19 Habermas, *Moral Consciousness*, 100.

20 Michigan in general, and Detroit and its suburb Dearborn in particular, has the highest percentage of people of Arab descent in the United States. At least 4 percent of Wayne County's population is of Arab descent, and 23 percent of the population of Dearborn speaks Arabic at home. The Arab community in Michigan is highly institutionalized and politically organized. Organizations like the Association of Arab University Graduates, which helped produce both the Arab American Institution and the American-Arab Anti-Discrimination Committee, were founded in Michigan. ACCESS (the Arab Community Center for Economic and Social Services) in Dearborn is the largest Arab American community organization in the country; the Arab American National Museum is an offshoot of it. Because of their numerical size, concentration in electoral units (especially Michigan's 12th electoral district), and high institutionalization, Arab Americans have made more inroads into electoral politics in Michigan than elsewhere nationwide.

21 For instance, Sobieraj and White, "Civic Engagement"; Bloemraad, *Becoming a Citizen*.

22 For instance, Kristi Andersen, "Parties, Organizations, and Political Incorporation: Immigrants in Six U.S. Cities," in *Civic Hopes and Political Realities: Im-*

migrants, Community Organizations, and Political Engagement, ed. S. Karthick
Ramakrishnan and Irene Bloemraad (New York: Russell Sage, 2008), 77–106;
Irene Bloemraad and S. Karthick Ramakrishnan, "Making Organizations Count:
Immigrant Civic Engagement in California Cities," in Ramakrishnan and Bloem-
raad, *Civic Hopes and Political Realities*, 45–76; Els de Graauw and Floris Vermeu-
len, "Cities and the Politics of Immigrant Integration: A Comparison of Berlin,
Amsterdam, New York City, and San Francisco," *Journal of Ethnic and Migration
Studies* 42, no. 6 (2016): 989–1012; Els de Graauw, *Making Immigrant Rights Real:
Nonprofits and the Politics of Integration in San Francisco* (Ithaca, NY: Cornell
University Press, 2016).

23 Hector Cordero-Guzmàn, "Community-Based Organizations and Immigration in
New York City," *Journal of Ethnic and Migration Studies* 31, no. 5 (2005): 889–909,
894.

24 Lisa Wedeen, "Ethnography as Interpretive Enterprise," in *Political Ethnography:
What Immersion Contributes to the Study of Power*, ed. Edward Schatz (Chicago:
University of Chicago Press, 2009), 75–94.

25 For my fellow political scientists engaged in the debates around methods-driven
and problem-driven political science, this strikes me as a clear example of the circu-
lar relationship between the topic of study and the methods chosen. In many ways,
my work is what Ian Shapiro would call problem driven, meaning that the problem
comes first and the methods are selected to provide the best answer. In the case of
this project, ethnography was the best method for me to capture and understand
how people talk about and conceptualize politics in contexts embedded in the
everyday life of Arab New York, so I chose to rely on it. At the same time, my desire
to ask my question this way, rather than some other way of understanding political
life in these communities, stems from the fact that I believe that research methods
that are deeply attentive to the everyday grant more purchase over what is actually
happening there than alternative processes. Rather than choosing a neutral question
from a pool of possible research topics, I chose this question because it strikes me as
superior. Clearly, my own preferences and frameworks as a researcher—and a political thinker, a person engaged in political life, as all of us are—contributed to my
choice of this "better question." So my choice of methods was not contingent merely
upon the framing of the particular research topic I wanted to engage in, but also
flowed from broader political and intellectual processes, which predisposed me to
seek out projects best understood through the logic of interpretive research. For all
of our calls for methodological ecumenicalism, researchers have preexisting preferences that it would be intellectually dishonest to ignore and that drive the questions
we use to frame our research and the methods we use to obtain answers.

26 Lorraine Bayard de Volo, "Participant Observation, Politics, and Power Relations:
Nicaraguan Mothers and U.S. Casino Waitresses," in Schatz, *Political Ethnography*,
217–236, 229.

27 I wrote an undergraduate thesis on feminist anti-occupation activism in Israel
and Palestine; through my fieldwork for that thesis, I became involved in support-

ing the work of the Israeli Women in Black, the Coalition of Women for a Just Peace, and other activist groups in Israel fighting the occupation. I then spent my time between finishing my undergraduate degree and beginning graduate school working as an activist/lobbyist for issues related to women and war, at the United Nations as an NGO representative and with activist groups; I also took community Arabic classes, which were attended by Palestine activists who were improving their language skills to support their work. So I entered the sphere of Palestine activism not as a total outsider but as someone who had been "out of the loop" for a good four years before coming back as a researcher and whose experiences had been shaped by the spheres of her prior work.

CHAPTER 2. MAPPING ARAB NEW YORK

1 The classic work on early Arab immigrants to the United States is Alixa Naff's *Becoming American: The Early Arab Immigrant Experience* (Carbondale: Southern Illinois University Press, 1993), although Hani Bardawi's *The Making of Arab Americans from Syrian Nationalism to U.S. Citizenship* (Austin: University of Texas Press, 2014) provides some needed further nuance on political organizing among these early arrivals, and Sarah Gualtieri's *Between Arab and White: Race and Ethnicity in the Early Syrian American Diaspora* (Berkeley: University of California Press, 2006) situates the community within early twentieth-century racial categorizations. For a focus on the 1970s through the 1990s, Michael Suleiman's edited collection *Arabs in America: Building a New Future* (Philadelphia: Temple University Press, 1999) brings together key authors and narratives, while Nabeel Abraham and Andrew Shryock's *Arab Detroit: From Margin to Mainstream* (Detroit: Wayne State University Press, 2000) provides detailed framings on local dynamics in southeastern Michigan that provide excellent grounding for understanding the later waves.

2 Arab American Institute Foundation, "Demographics," www.aaiusa.org.

3 For some examples of this quantitative work, see Karam Dana, Kassra A. R. Oskooii, and Matt A. Barreto, "Mosques as American Institutions: Mosque Attendance, Religiosity and Integration into the Political System among American Muslims," *Religions* 2, no. 4 (2011): 504–524; Detroit Arab American Study Team, *Citizenship and Crisis: Arab Detroit after 9/11* (New York: Russell Sage Foundation, 2009); Amaney Jamal, "The Political Participation and Engagement of Muslim Americans: Mosque Involvement and Group Consciousness," *American Politics Research* 33, no. 4 (2005): 521–544; Jen'nan Ghazal Read, *Culture, Class, and Work among Arab-American Women* (New York: LFB, 2004).

4 All American Community Survey (ACS) statistics are from the 2010–2012 three-year estimates, unless otherwise noted. These estimates are derived from rounds of the survey conducted during and immediately after the period of my fieldwork; I use the three-year estimates to compensate for the small number of people of Arab descent in the sample, as suggested by the Census Bureau. For more information on the ACS and greater details on these questions, visit http://factfinder.

census.gov. For any researchers looking to perform tests of statistical association
with regard to Arab Americans in the ACS, I recommend retrieving an IPUMS
(Integrated Public Use Microdata Series) sample from http://ipums.org, which
can provide random samples of ACS data to be used for analysis in standard
statistical software. Arab and other Middle Eastern ancestry codes are located in
the 400s.

5 Approximately half of Jordan's population, including Queen Rania, wife of the
current monarch, is Palestinian by ethnicity; unlike other Arab countries, Jordan
granted citizenship to Palestinians who settled there after 1948. There has been
some intermarriage between "East-Bankers" and Palestinians in urban communities, but Palestinian refugee camps still exist, and the nonurban, "tribal" portion
of Jordanian society is socially and legally privileged. A substantial proportion of
Israel's population is of Arab descent, either Palestinian Muslims or Christians,
or Jews from throughout the Arab world, particularly Yemen, Morocco, Iraq, and
Egypt. However, the extent to which Mizrahi (Arab/Middle Eastern descended)
Jews outside of Israel identify as Arab or Middle Eastern is unclear to me and
has not, to my knowledge, been studied. For an introduction to the dynamics of
Mizrahi identifications in the Israeli and Middle Eastern contexts, see Ella Shohat,
"The Invention of the Mizrahim," *Journal of Palestine Studies* 29, no. 1 (1999): 5–
20.

6 It is worth reminding the reader that these data come from before the rollout
of the marketplaces required by the Affordable Care Act ("Obamacare"), and so
private purchase was fairly limited.

7 Only Brooklyn and Queens have enough Arab residents for consistent statistics
on these questions, but in the ACS 2010 five-year sample, 3.7 percent of Arab
Manhattanites, 13.6 percent of Arabs in the Bronx, and 8.3 percent of Arabs
in Staten Island received SNAP benefits. In Manhattan, those living under the
poverty line represented 13.3 percent of Arab families and 25.8 percent of Arab
children; in the Bronx, 22.3 percent of families and 41.3 percent of children; in
Staten Island, 11.0 percent of families and 10.9 percent of children.

8 John R. Logan, Richard D. Alba, and Wenquan Zhang, "Immigrant Enclaves
and Ethnic Communities in New York and Los Angeles," *American Sociological
Review* 67, no. 2 (2002): 299–322, 311.

9 Fourth Avenue Presbyterian no longer has a majority of Arab worshippers,
although the older generation is still largely of Arab descent and the names of
their parents and grandparents are recorded in stained glass windows and other
memorabilia of the history of the congregation.

10 Iris Marion Young, "State, Civil Society, and Social Justice," in *Democracy's Values*,
ed. Ian Shapiro and Casiano Hacker-Cordón (Cambridge: Cambridge University
Press, 1999), 141–162, 145–148.

11 Linda's own personal trajectory has gotten increasingly political over the years
since my research, including leadership in the Muslim Democratic Committee
of New York and MPower Change, a national Muslim social justice coalition, a

prominent role in Bernie Sanders's presidential campaign, and leadership of the 2017 Women's March. As of this writing, she has announced she is leaving the AAA-NY to focus on national politics.

12 For an overview of the literature on social capital and political behavior, see Dietlind Stolle, "Social Capital," in *The Oxford Handbook of Political Behavior*, ed. Russell J. Dalton and Hans-Dieter Klingemann (Oxford: Oxford University Press, 2007), 655–674.

13 Young, "State, Civil Society, and Social Justice," 148–153.

14 See, for example, Deborah Reed-Danahay and Caroline B. Brettell, "'Communities of Practice' for Civic and Political Engagement: Asian Indian and Vietnamese Immigrant Organizations in a Southwest Metropolis," in Civic Hopes and Political Realities: Immigrants, Community Organizations, and Political Engagement, ed. S. Karthick Ramakrishnan and Irene Bloemraad (New York: Russell Sage, 2008), 195–221; Hector Cordero-Guzmàn, "Community-Based Organizations and Immigration in New York City," Journal of Ethnic and Migration Studies 31, no. 5 (2005): 889–909; Janelle Wong, *Democracy's Promise: Immigrants and American Civic Institutions* (Ann Arbor: University of Michigan Press, 2006).

15 Arab American Association of New York, "Our Mission," www.arabamericanny.org/our-mission/.

16 Stockton, "Arab-American Political Participation."

17 Nadine Naber, *Arab America: Gender, Cultural Politics, and Activism* (New York: New York University Press, 2012).

18 For instance, Ramakrishnan's meticulous comparative work found that only 12–16 percent of first-generation immigrants, 13–18 percent of second-generation immigrants, and 8–19 percent of people in the third generation and beyond attended a protest or electoral rally in the 2002 electoral cycle in California, whereas 32–66 percent of all generations voted, 31–45 percent attended local community meetings, and 23–47 percent signed a petition. See S. Karthick Ramakrishnan, *Democracy in Immigrant America: Changing Demographics and Political Participation* (Stanford, CA: Stanford University Press, 2005).

19 I owe the first articulation of this insight to an Adalah-NY member, who during an early interview spoke about Adalah-NY's difficulty in organizing in Bay Ridge and elaborated upon this distinction.

20 It is worth explaining why I chose to continue my research on Al-Awda when leadership expressed disinterest, while I stopped research on the AAFSC when it acted likewise. My choice was based on the difference in the publicness of the actions of the groups. The AAFSC's public actions were fairly limited; their central purpose was to act as a professional social service organization, and they did not organize events or publicize information about the organization or its clients, apart from limited PR work. (In fact, the AAA did more public-facing events at the time than the AAFSC did.) The work that the AAFSC did that interested me was conducted in private, by which I mean in places that admitted only certain authorized participants and kept others out. I did not have access to that informa-

tion, nor could I find a route to it without permission and cooperation. However, as Al-Awda was an activist group, a huge proportion of its events were public, intended to be seen and understood not only by participants but by nonpartici-pants. There could be no reasonable expectation of privacy during these events; in fact, there was an expectation not only of publicness but of publicity, of the idea that what happened would be spread further. Although a great deal of potentially useful data was lost to me by not observing how Al-Awda worked internally, and how members and leaders made choices and prioritized actions, plenty was publicly available in the form of observations of their actions. Therefore, I was able to carry out the comparative research that interested me, both ethically and practically, in the case of Palestine activism.

CHAPTER 3. MAKING ʿARABIYA

1 Hannah Arendt, *Between Past and Future* (New York: Penguin, 1977), 119.

2 Courtney Jung, "Race, Ethnicity, Religion," in *The Oxford Handbook of Contex-tual Political Analysis*, ed. Robert E. Goodin and Charles Tilly (Oxford: Oxford University Press, 2006), 370.

3 For an introduction to the politics of pan-Arabism and related frameworks, see Nazih Ayubi, *Over-stating the Arab State: Politics and Society in the Middle East* (New York: I.B. Tauris, 1995).

4 Katherine Cramer Walsh, *Talking about Politics: Informal Groups and Social Iden-tity in American Life* (Chicago: University of Chicago Press, 2004), 4.

5 *Hummus* is the Arabic word for chickpeas; the spread is known as *hummus bi tahineh* (chickpeas with sesame paste).

6 Or by my pronunciation, or maybe just my putting it on a sandwich made of American bread.

7 Almost all of the children had at least one sibling in the program, and in one case there were two pairs of cousins who arrived together and shared lunch.

8 *Koshary* is an Egyptian macaroni and lentil dish. *Lahme* literally means meat; *lahme bi ajeen* (meat on dough) is a meat pie common in the Levant.

9 At one point he actually joked, "We Arabs need to come up with some new names."

CHAPTER 4. THE PANOPTICON OF BAY RIDGE

1 It is worth pointing out that members of majority communities also have "cultural practices," which can be equally as misogynist and patriarchal; a woman who chooses to leave behind minority cultural practices because she finds them stifling enters into majority cultural practices, which she may find more agreeable, but are no less a set of gendered constraints. There is no neutral, culture-free space of liberty: only choices among varieties and strategies for resistance or accommoda-tion.

2 The use of the term "girl" can be fraught for many Anglophone feminists, who see its use as infantilizing toward those beyond puberty; the teenagers I talk

about in this chapter would be best called, on that analysis, "young women." But in majority Arab usage, to call an unmarried female person a woman (and not a girl) would be to imply that she was sexually active, a major violation of gender norms. In general in this chapter, I refer to those of high school age as girls, which best represents their self-understanding, while those of college age and older I call young women.

3 As the organization professionalized, the percentage of staff who are Arab Americans from Bay Ridge has shrunk and more staff hold college degrees, rather than being college students (or even high school students, as with some of the staff I worked with).

4 Leadership in Adalah-NY is mixed-gender, and participants in the group have a general progressive orientation that includes a form of feminism. In fact, two of the non-Arab women members have strong roots in the feminist antiwar movement, making institutional linkages between issues of gender and Palestinian liberation. However, because Adalah-NY's members, Arab and non-Arab, are not deeply integrated into Bay Ridge or immigrant communities in general, I do not discuss them in this chapter.

5 Many young married women and some unmarried girls cover, but uncovered women are also a major part of the community organization scene in Bay Ridge.

6 In fact, education is prized for both male and female children in middle-class Arab communities in both the United States and the Middle East; even the most patriarchal families frequently believe that an educated daughter will command a better marriage partner and will raise better children, or at least that education is a fine way for a daughter to spend her time before marriage; girls who marry in college frequently negotiate with their husbands and in-laws to finish their degrees.

7 Michel Foucault, *Discipline and Punish: The Birth of the Prison* (New York: Vintage, 1979), 251–252.

8 Ibid., 178–179.

9 Ibid., 27–28.

10 Of the women I taught in the ESL program, for instance, all of them covered, with three exceptions: one began covering while attending the program, one was Christian, and one was much younger than the others. All the married Muslim women with children covered. Only two of the women in the ESL program wore Western clothes with hijab.

11 All three were anti-Zionist: an Arab (but not Palestinian) imam, a Palestinian priest, and a rabbi from Neturai Karta; see chapter 5 for more information on the dynamics of Palestine movements in New York.

12 The norms in non-Muslim Arab communities are similar to those in Arab Muslim communities, but not identical.

13 For an excellent treatment of the dynamics of seeing and being seen, dating, romance, and religious norms among Muslim university students, see Shabana Mir, Muslim American Women on Campus: Undergraduate Social Life and Identity,

University of North Carolina Press, especially Chapter 5, "Let Them Be Normal and Date: Muslim American Undergraduate Women in Sexualized Campus Culture, pp. 126-172.

14 "Enthusiastic consent" is a term recently developed by feminist activists and writers to emphasize that the standard for ethical sexual conduct should be that all parties actively and without constraint give their consent; that is, rather defining rape as "someone said no," we should define non-rape as "everyone said yes."

15 Rose ended up attending a school within the City University of New York system.

16 Most of these girls eventually dropped out of the Brooklynat; in the analysis of the staff organizing the group, they seemed more interested in socializing than in community service and activism.

CHAPTER 5. FROM THE EAST RIVER TO THE SEA

1 It is worth nothing that there are also pro-Israel activists, mostly but not exclusively Jewish, who prefer a one-state solution and support tactics that are distasteful to Americans who do not have a strong political association with a "Greater Israel" ideology, such as financially supporting settlements.

2 For the history of the meanings of the kuffiyeh, see Ted Swedenberg, "Seeing Double: Palestinian-American Histories of the Kufiya," *Michigan Quarterly Review* 31, no. 4 (1992): 557–577.

3 For more information, see BBC, "Gaza-Bound Aid Convoy Leaving UK," February 14, 2009, http://news.bbc.co.uk; Haroon Siddique, "George Galloway Deported from Egypt," *Guardian*, January 8, 2010, www.theguardian.com. The first Gaza Freedom Flotilla, held in May 2010, was an attempt to deliver humanitarian aid to Gaza without passing through Israeli customs. It ended in a disastrous Israeli raid on the largest ships, sponsored by a Turkish Islamic humanitarian relief organization, and the death of nine Turkish activists. It has been followed by a number of other Freedom Flotillas, in 2011, 2015, and 2018. For more information, see Isabel Kershner, "Defying Blockage, Cargo and Passenger Vessels Head for Gaza," *New York Times*, May 27, 2010, www.nytimes.com; Ian Black and Haroon Siddique, "Q&A: The Gaza Freedom Flotilla," *Guardian*, May 31, 2010.

4 Interestingly, it was "Mawtini" ("My Homeland"), a historic anthem based on a poem by Ibrahim Tuqan, that was sung, rather than "Fida'i" (a word best translated as "guerilla fighter" or "freedom fighter" in this context), the anthem of the Palestinian National Authority.

5 Omar Barghouti, "Putting Palestine Back on the Map: Boycott as Civil Resistance," *Journal of Palestine Studies* 35, no. 3 (2006): 51–57.

6 *Sumud* is literally steadfastness, a rhetorical concept with deep resonance in Palestinian politics that praises Palestinians for continuing to exist in the face of Israeli occupation.

7 See, for instance, Jake Miller, "Black Viewpoints on the Mid-East Conflict," *Journal of Palestine Studies* 10, no. 2 (1981): 37–49; Alfred T. Moleah, "Violations

of Palestinian Human Rights: South African Parallels," *Journal of Palestine Studies* 10, no. 2 (1981): 14–36; Robert G. Newby, "Afro-Americans and Arabs: An Alliance in the Making?," *Journal of Palestine Studies* 10, no. 2 (1981): 50–58; Lewis Young, "American Blacks and the Arab-Israeli Conflict," *Journal of Palestine Studies* 2, no. 1 (1972): 70–85.

8 Calling for *takbir* is the praising of God, which is commonly used in place of applause by strict Muslims. The speaker calls out *Takbir!* and the audience responds *Allahu akbar. Bismillah ar-rahman ar-rahim,* "in the name of God, the Merciful, the Compassionate," is the first line of each chapter of the Qur'an and is regularly said before speech or action to invoke God's presence, to give support to the speaker, or to simply mark the beginning of a formal presentation.

9 The rough statistics divide Muslims in American three major categories, the largest group South Asian in origin, with black Muslims and Arab Muslims only slightly smaller. Of course there are also Muslims of all races and ethnicities, due to conversion and the worldwide spread of Islam.

10 These sorts of barriers are common in pro-Palestine organizing. The meeting I attended was the last open gathering Adalah-NY held for the foreseeable future; several months later, it switched to a model of doing one-on-one orientations in advance of meetings, to bring new members in without needing to wait for an open meeting.

11 I was one of the new attenders who had previous experience, both from my prior involvement as a student activist and from my research on and participation in the feminist anti-occupation movement in Israel/Palestine.

12 See, for example, Cynthia Cockburn, *From Where We Stand: War, Women's Activism and Feminist Analysis* (London: Zed Books, 2007); Susan Munkres, "Being 'Sisters' to Salvadoran Peasants: Deep Identification and Its Limitations," in *Identity Work in Social Movements,* ed. Jo Reger, Daniel J. Myers, and Rachel L. Einwohner (Minneapolis: University of Minnesota Press, 2008), 189–212; Simona Sharoni, *Gender and the Israeli-Palestinian Conflict: The Politics of Women's Resistance* (Syracuse, NY: Syracuse University Press, 1995).

13 The full text is available at https://bdsmovement.net/call.

14 Bil'in is a key site for activism against the appropriation of Palestinian land by Israel in the course of building what Palestinians call the "Apartheid Wall" as well as a well-networked community for international visitors. For instance, at the International Meeting of the Women in Black I attended in 2005, the international women were taken for a tour of Bil'in and to attend their weekly protest, and the US LGBT Delegation to Palestine also visited the village.

15 Andrew Boyd, "Irony, Meme Warfare, and the Extreme Costume Ball," in *From Act Up to the WTO: Urban Protest and Community Building in the Era of Globalization,* ed. Benjamin Shepard and Ronald Hayduk (New York: Verso, 2002), 250.

16 The concepts of bonding and bridging social capital were first articulated in Robert Putnam, *Bowling Alone: The Collapse and Revival of American Community* (New York: Simon & Schuster, 2000).

17 Manuel Castells, *The Power of Identity* (Malden, MA: Blackwell, 1997).

18 Full disclosure: I was a member of Park Slope Food Co-op at the time the BDS conversation began, but I did not vote in the decision.

CHAPTER 6. *THAWRA FII* TIMES SQUARE

1 Egyptian Association for Change USA, "About Us," https://web.archive.org/web/20110428230207/, www.eacusa.org/about-eacusa.html (via the Internet Archive's Wayback Machine).

2 For details on #Right2Vote, see Marta Severo and Eleonora Zuolo, "Egyptian e-Diaspora: Migrant Websites without a Network?," *Social Science Information* 51, no. 4 (December 2012): 521–533.

3 Yemeni American Coalition for Change, "About Us," http://yaccny.org.

4 Yossi Shain, *Kinship and Diaspora in International Relations* (Ann Arbor: University of Michigan Press, 2007); Latha Varadarajan, *The Domestic Abroad: Diasporas in International Relations* (New York: Oxford University Press, 2010).

5 Luis Eduardo Guarnizo, Alejandro Portes, and William Haller, "Assimilation and Transnationalism: Determinants of Transnational Political Action among Contemporary Migrants," *American Journal of Sociology* 108, no. 6 (2003): 1211–1248.

6 Alejandro Portes, Cristina Escobar, and Renelinda Arana, "Bridging the Gap: Transnational and Ethnic Organizations in the Political Incorporation of Immigrants in the United States," *Ethnic and Racial Studies* 31, no. 6 (2008): 1056–1090.

7 Ange-Marie Hancock, "When Multiplication Doesn't Equal Quick Addition: Examining Intersectionality as a Research Paradigm," *Perspectives on Politics* 5, no. 1 (2007): 63–79.

8 Kimberlé Crenshaw, "Mapping the Margins: Intersectionality, Identity Politics, and Violence Against Women of Color," *Stanford Law Review* 43, no. 6 (1991): 1241–1299.

9 A good account of the claims can be found in the *Arab American News* article "Scandal Rocks ADC: Sexual Harassment Allegations Against Civil Rights Advocate Shocks Community," June 7, 2013, www.arabamericannews.com.

10 The now-offline website KABOBFest held a vigorous debate on the Jandali controversy. Two key essays are Will Tanzman's piece in favor of engaging for change with the ADC, available on the Internet Archive at http://web.archive.org/web/20110614160304/, www.kabobfest.com/2011/06/the-adc-challenge.html, and Sarab Al-Jijakli's set of demands to the organization, available on the Internet Archive at http://web.archive.org/web/20160925050201/, www.kabobfest.com/2011/06/demands-for-change-at-adc-this-weekend.html.

11 SCAF is the Supreme Council of the Armed Forces, the military government that ruled Egypt between the ouster of Mubarak and the election of Morsi.

12 For a brief survey of the history of diaspora political organizing and state efforts to enlist diasporas to support their social goals, see Fiona B. Adamson, "The Growing Importance of Diaspora Politics," *Current History*, November 2016, 291–297.

13 Yossi Shain, "Ethnic Diasporas and U.S. Foreign Policy," *Political Science Quarterly* 190, no. 5 (1994): 811–841, 817–818. Interestingly, his analysis in the same article of African American diaspora engagement toward South Africa and other sub-Saharan African countries is much more nuanced.

14 Ibid., 832.

15 Muhammad Bilal Lakhani, "Thursday Evening: At the Mosque, Anger," *Brooklyn Ink*, February 4, 2011, http://thebrooklynink.com.

16 "NY-Area Egyptians Celebrate Mubarak's Departure," *New York Post*, February 11, 2011, http://blogs.wsj.com.

17 Shavana Abruzzo, "Marty's Flies the Flag of Solidarity for the People of Egypt," *New York Post*, March 1, 2011, www.nypost.com.

CONCLUSION

1 It shouldn't be surprising, then, that feminist political theory has been at the fore-front of demonstrating the deeply political nature of personal relationships—an argument central to the work of Susan Moller Okin, Nancy Fraser, and countless others. Power, politics, and gender intersect in the sphere of everyday relations more than anywhere else and with the farthest-reaching consequences.

2 The poll, "American Attitudes toward Arabs, Muslims, Immigration, Civil Rights, and Surveillance (July 2017)," can be accessed online at the Arab American Institute's website, www.aaiusa.org.

3 The poll, "Arab American Voters 2016: Identity and Political Concerns," can be accessed online at the Arab American Institute's website, www.aaiusa.org.

4 For instance, I know every time she is mentioned in the news because my aunt, who met Sarsour when they were both members of the New York State Sanders Caucus at the 2016 Democratic National Convention, sends me a Facebook message that she saw a story about "my friend."

5 Stephen Salaita, *The Uncultured Wars: Arabs, Muslims, and the Poverty of Liberal Thought-New Essays* (New York: St. Martin's, 2008).

INDEX

ABOUT THE AUTHOR

Emily Regan Wills is Associate Professor of Comparative and American Politics at the University of Ottawa. She co-directs the Community Mobilization in Crisis project, documenting and supporting community organizing and mobilization in the Arab world, and researches transnational social processes in the Middle East. Her roots are in queer, feminist, and antiwar organizing.